BRIGHT NOTES

CALL OF THE WILD AND WHITE FANG BY JACK LONDON

Intelligent Education

Nashville, Tennessee

BRIGHT NOTES: Call of the Wild and White Fang
www.BrightNotes.com

No part of this publication may be used or reproduced in any manner whatsoever without written permission, except in the case of brief quotations in critical articles and reviews. For permissions, contact Influence Publishers http://www.influencepublishers.com.

ISBN: 978-1-645422-36-5 (Paperback)
ISBN: 978-1-645422-37-2 (eBook)

Published in accordance with the U.S. Copyright Office Orphan Works and Mass Digitization report of the register of copyrights, June 2015.

Originally published by Monarch Press.
Donald F. Roden; W John Campbell, 1965
2020 Edition published by Influence Publishers.

Interior design by Lapiz Digital Services. Cover Design by Thinkpen Designs.

Printed in the United States of America.

Library of Congress Cataloging-in-Publication Data forthcoming.
Names: Intelligent Education
Title: BRIGHT NOTES: Call of the Wild and White Fang
Subject: STU004000 STUDY AIDS / Book Notes

CONTENTS

1)	Introduction to Jack London	1
2)	Textual Analysis	8
	Chapter I	8
	Chapter II	14
	Chapter III	19
	Chapter IV	26
	Chapter V	31
	Chapter VI	37
	Chapter VII	42
3)	Essay Questions And Answers	53
4)	Textual Analysis	57
	Chapters I-III	57
	Chapters IV-VIII	60
	Chapter IX	63
	Chapter X	65
	Chapters XI-XII	67
	Chapter XIII	69
	Chapter XIV	71
	Chapter XV	73
	Chapter XVI	75

	Chapters XVII-XVIII	78
	Chapter XIX	81
	Chapter XX	83
	Chapters XXI-XXIII	85
	Chapter XXIV	87
	Chapter XXV	89
5)	Character Analysis And Theme	90
6)	Essay Questions And Answers	93
7)	Critical Commentary	95
8)	Bibliography	99

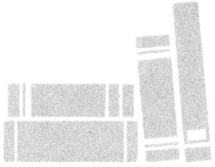

CALL OF THE WILD AND WHITE FANG

INTRODUCTION TO JACK LONDON

BIOGRAPHIC COMMENT

Jack London was born in San Francisco in 1876. The product of a broken home and a poverty-stricken family, he left school at the age of fourteen to go to work. In those times, this was not an unusual occurrence for an average boy, because then school was not considered the necessity that we think it to be nowadays. However, the things that Jack London did were unusual. While still in his teens, he shipped as an able seaman to Japan and the Siberian coast and also worked with a group of oyster pirates. He took odd jobs in mills and a canning factory, and worked his way across the country with a group of socialists who had planned a march on Washington to protest conditions among the poor. Then he joined the gold-rush. He later went to Japan as a war correspondent in 1904 and to Mexico in 1914. He died at age forty.

LONDON LEGEND

Wound up with the facts of Jack London's life there is much legend. It is a fact that in 1897, when he was twenty-one-years old, he went to the Klondike with the first rush of gold-seekers. Much fable is mixed up with the stories of what he did there, however. Many people believe that London personally saw and did everything that he wrote about in his adventurous stories. Others doubt that he ever did any of these things himself. Somewhere in between is the truth, although the whole of it will probably never be known. There is no doubt, however, that he did follow the rush into the Klondike, that his experience with boats helped him in crossing the dangerous Whitehorse Rapids, that he did stake a claim, but that a year later he returned home as poor as when he had left.

AUTOBIOGRAPHICAL NOVEL

Our study of the life of Jack London is further complicated by the novel Martin Eden, which was published in 1909. This book is what is termed an autobiographical novel-that is, based on the actual life of its author-but how much of it is true and how much is false we do not know for sure. It is the fiction author's privilege to do with truth whatever he thinks necessary for the creation of a good narrative. Also, besides being a novelist, Jack London looked upon himself as something of a social philosopher, and he used this story as a means of showing the effect that his ideas about life had or should have had upon the life of his central character. Martin Eden, therefore, cannot truly be considered as the real Jack London in the things he did or said. He is only the Jack London that the author saw himself as being. This novel, then, should not in every sense be taken as literally true, and should be considered only as a help in the study of the author's life.

EDUCATION

Though poorly educated, Jack London had a tremendous respect for the value of education. This respect was undoubtedly gained in large measure during the years immediately following his leaving school. After wandering about the country and drifting from job to job, he realized that he was not getting anywhere, and that he was still as poor as ever. Not wanting to take the time to return to high school, he crammed enough knowledge into his head during a three-month period of reading and study so that he was able to pass a special entrance examination for college. He enrolled at the University of California; but, after a few months, the lure of the "gold rush" got him, and he was off to the Klondike in 1897.

WRITING CAREER

When Jack London returned home a year later, he began to put his energy into the task of writing. Success did not come to him immediately. He spent the next years writing stories, begging publishers to accept them, and receiving as little as five dollars for them when they would be accepted. In 1900, the first volume of his collected short stories appeared in a book called *The Son of the Wolf*. Included in this volume is the famous "Odyssey of the North." However, *The Call of the Wild*, published in 1903, which brought fame to the author and which led to his being one of the most financially successful writers of his time. This novel was then followed by *The Sea Wolf* (1904), *White Fang* (1906), *Martin Eden* (1909), plus numerous short stories and political essays. Before his death in 1916, he had published forty-nine volumes.

SOCIAL BACKGROUND

With Jack London, as with many authors, we can really understand his writings only in the light of his own times. And what was these times? First of all, and most importantly, it was the height of the Industrial Revolution in American society when the barons of industry held free sway. In 1882, for instance, John D. Rockefeller established the Standard Oil Trust, a group of some forty oil companies, and used every cutthroat method to suppress competition. Then, in 1892, Andrew Carnegie, the great steel magnate, used hired thugs to break up a strike among his workers. There was no effective legislation on the side of the laboring man. It would seem that even the federal government was opposed to the Labor Movement, for in 1877, President Hayes, and in 1894, President Cleveland, each sent out Federal troops to quell riots which had arisen during railroad strikes. These were indeed times of economic turmoil.

LONDON'S SOCIALISM

There were other factors which made those restless times. For instance, a great influx of non-English speaking immigrants was flooding the labor market and making it easier for the industrialists to keep salaries and working conditions at whatever low standards they desired. Opposed to these unfair practices of management was the rising wave of socialism which had a statement of doctrine in Karl Marx's Das Kapital, and which, under the direction of men like Eugene Debs, was advocating violence and revolution instead of peaceful legislation and order as the means by which the laboring man in the United States should better himself.

Young Jack London, poor himself, as was pointed out before, and forced to go to work at an early age in order to support himself, became an advocate of this violent type of socialism-class warfare, revolution, and the overthrow of the capitalist by the laboring class. He preached it loudly on the street corners, and a little more quietly in his books. On one occasion he allowed himself to be arrested in order to test the legality of an Oakland, California, law; and on more than one occasion he signed his letters "Yours for the Revolution."

PHILOSOPHY

We have said that Jack London was a socialist in his political thinking. His writings reflect this; but more importantly they also are deliberate attempts to explain the philosophy of naturalism. This is the theory that man's entire life is controlled by his environment. London was a voracious reader, and one of his favorite authors was Herbert Spencer. Now Spencer is the one perhaps most responsible for spreading the theory of evolution that man is descended from lower forms of life. In *The Call of the Wild* London traces the steps by which a tame or civilized dog retraces the evolutionary steps until he finds himself in his original primitive state. In *White Fang* the process is reversed. The half-wolf rises from his wild, primitive state to one of civilization. But Jack London's was an undisciplined mind. He read only what he wanted to read and believed only what he wanted to believe. Even these two books, then, which most critics consider his best, have a certain vagueness about them. Mixed with the naturalism is a romanticism, an escapism which carries the reader away from the reality of his surroundings into the adventuresome wilderness of the Klondike. Also in the naturalism a definite lack of purpose is evident. The reader is forced to ask himself at the end of each of these novels: Is London really serious about wanting us to believe that we have no control over our environment or over our destiny?

THE MAN

Jack London as a man is an enigma. He was the embodiment of the ideal early twentieth-century American-romantic, vigorous, a self-educated success. Also he was an ardent disciple of both socialism and evolution. However, like many of his kind, he was also proud, naive, and indecisive. His voracious reading did not lead him down a road of satisfied contentment. Instead it led him through a wilderness of doubt from which he did not seem able to find the means of escape. He died of uremic poisoning according to the four physicians in attendance at his bedside.

THE CALL OF THE WILD

Anyone who picks up this novel expecting an animal story in the tradition of *Black Beauty* or *My Friend Flicka* is in for a disappointment. Told from the point of view of the dog Buck, this story, as other animal stories, contains a great amount of sentimentalism. However, unlike other animal stories, it contains a great amount of brutality, viciousness, and disregard for the value of human life. The dog Buck is the only really important thing in the novel. His survival is what counts. The other dogs, and even the humans in the story, are merely a background against which the story of this survival takes place. They can pass out of the picture without explanation or without reason. For example, at the end of Chapter 5, the ice breaks away under Charles, Hal, and Mercedes, carrying them to their death. None of these people has done anything worthy of this cruel death, unless it be that they were mean to Buck. Moreover, John Thornton expresses sympathy only for Buck and not for the victims of this tragedy.

The law of the "club and the fang" is the predominant element in this novel. Kill or be killed is what drags Buck relentlessly through his adventures until finally he is released from any hold that civilization has upon him. At the conclusion of the story, he is not only with the wolf pack; he is one of them.

The Call of the Wild is not really a novel in the strict sense that we think of *Silas Marner* or *David Copperfield* as being novels. Rather it is more like seven distinct short stories, each with its own characters, its own plot and **climax**. Buck runs though each of them, with each being an **episode** in the story of his return to the primitive state. Through each chapter relies on the other for continuity, each could almost be read separately and be appreciated for itself. Thus, from this point of view, we have an interesting situation as you will see in our chapter-by-chapter discussion of the work.

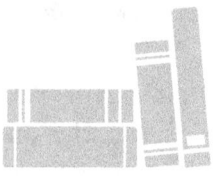

CALL OF THE WILD

TEXTUAL ANALYSIS

CHAPTER I

This chapter, entitled "Into the Primitive," begins with a verse of four lines which introduces the reader to the **theme** of the novel. Buried within the individual is a ferine* strain, a bestial instinct, which has been subdued by the customs of our civilization. This instinct, however, is not dead but sleeping. It is a "brumal sleep," a winter's hibernation similar to that of the bear, for instance, whose bestiality is completely subdued during this time. However, the force still exists; and when awakened, it can be seen again in all its natural ferocity.

Comment

As we read this story, we will see a change come over Buck, a change which is gradual but natural. At first he is the big playful dog much like those we have around our own homes. However,

---
* ferine-animal

as the story progresses, we shall see all this disappear and Buck become a vicious animal.

Buck was born and lived on a huge estate which belonged to Judge Miller and his family. The house was the center of this estate which was covered with lawns and trees, grape arbors, orchards, and berry patches. In a word, it was the elegant home of a wealthy man, a place of luxury and ease.

Comment

If the reader is going to appreciate the contrasts of the story, there are two important facts that he should remember about the short description of the home where Buck spent his early years. The first of these is that the estate is a spacious place where nature exists in a controlled state. Note the author's simple but exact descriptions, such as interlacing boughs of tall poplars, vine clad cottages, and green pastures. Then the reader should note this second fact. This is not the home of an ordinary, or common, person. It is the home of the unusual person, the rich man.

The next picture that Jack London presents to us in the first chapter of this book is that of Buck as the king of Judge Miller's estate. Buck's father was Elmo, a huge St. Bernard which had been the inseparable companion of the Judge; and his mother was Shep, a Scotch shepherd. Also Buck had the run of the grounds, and on them he could do anything or go anywhere that he desired.

Comment

The author's use of apt expressions and his ability to say much in a few words is seen in this passage. Note the repeated use of the words king and royal. Note also the expression "a sated* aristocrat**." The cynicism of Jack London can be seen particularly in the line that tells us that Buck was perhaps even "a trifle egotistical***, as country gentlemen sometimes become because of their insular position." We have here a picture of Buck that will contrast with the later developments of the story. Buck is now the lord of the manor, living a life of luxury. He is respected by all, both animal and human.

The description of the kidnapping of Buck is told in a simple but meaningful, manner. The dog has learned to trust those he knows. Thus he goes willingly with Manuel, one of the gardeners helpers, and even allows Manuel to tie him. But the stranger he resents and shows this by springing at him. Here Buck learns his first lesson in primitive fighting, for the stranger merely grapples him by the throat and twists the rope tightly about his neck until the fight is gone out of him. The next thing of which Buck is aware is the shriek of the locomotive which is carrying him away from home. Once more he attacks his kidnapper and once more he is subdued. When he is taken off the train at San Francisco, Buck is brought to a saloon. Here the last vestige of civilization is removed from Buck as his collar is chiseled off, and he is flung into a cagelike crate.

---

* sated-satisfied

** aristocrat-a member of the privileged upper class

*** egotistical-self-centered

Comment

In this section of the story we see the quiet dignity of the dog Buck change into animal ferocity. The instinct for self-preservation manifests itself in the dog's ferocious attacks upon his captor. Also, although Buck's outward connection with civilization, his collar, is taken away, his inward connection still remains; for every time he hears the shed door rattle, he looks up expectantly for the Judge or the boys. His disappointment is shown as his joyful bark is turned into a savage growl.

From the saloon in San Francisco Buck was taken by train to Seattle. Although he is freed from the rope. Buck is unable to accustom himself to his new surroundings. He sulks, neither eats nor drinks, and becomes as a wild animal with blood-red eyes. At Seattle, Buck is delivered to the man in the red sweater. It is he who teaches Buck the first law of the wilderness, the law of the club. A vicious battle between the man and the dog takes place in which the dog is beaten. Here Buck learns that he is no match for a man with a club. After the fight, he submits and eats his food right out of the man's hand.

Comment

In this section of the story, the reader should note the author's use of the adjective red. Buck's eyes become a blood red and the man is wearing a red sweater. The symbolism here is not obscure, but it is important. Red is the color of blood, but it also represents animal savagery. At the hands of the man wearing the red sweater-himself something of a savage-Buck has learned the first law of the wilderness. The beating causes Buck to become covered with blood. However, the author notes, Buck is only beaten; he is not broken. When he eats from the hand of his conqueror, it is only because he knows that he is beaten. He has learned that the club represents primitive law and is something to be respected.

Now that Buck has learned the first hard law of the primitive, he is ready to move on to the North. At this point in the story, Perrault, a swarthy French-Canadian, comes into the life of the dog. An expert on the subject, he recognizes that Buck is one dog in a thousand, so he buys him and also a good-natured Newfoundland named Curly. Both dogs are taken aboard the Narwhal to set sail for the North. Below decks the dogs are put into the care of Francois, a half-breed. This man soon proves to Buck that he is fair, for when a big white dog from Spitzenbergen tries to steal from Buck's food, Francois cracks him with the whip. After several days at sea, uneasy ones for the dogs, the ship finally lands in the North, and Buck gets his first taste of snow.

Comment

In this part of the story, Buck is introduced to a new type of man represented by Perrault and Francois. They are men of the North whose very lives depend upon their dogs. Consequently, these men are neither friends nor enemies to any of the dogs, but treat each in a fair yet impersonal way. This point is illustrated by the incident of the attempted theft of food. Francois shows that he cannot permit trouble among the dogs by whipping Spitz. Also in this part of the story, Buck is introduced to a new element of nature-snow. He licked some on his tongue. "It bit like fire, and the next instant was gone." He is now beginning his struggle with nature.

Character Analysis

Buck: Although he is a dog, Buck represents mankind. In this first chapter, we see him as a self-satisfied member of a warm-climate, civilized society. Suddenly he is removed from this environment and forced to fight for survival. He gradually changes with each new experience.

The Judge: He is merely mentioned in the story. However, he represents the easy life of the warm Southland.

Manuel: He is important first of all because he is the one who kidnaps and sells Buck. However, more important, he represents the greed of civilized man. His wages are not sufficient to support both his family and his gambling. Thus he feels it is necessary to steal to get what he wants.

The Man In The Red Sweater: He is Buck's first real enemy. In the story, however, he is a transition character; for, although he lives in society with civilized man, he is, in reality, part of the uncivilized wilderness. It is he who teaches Buck the primitive law of the club.

Perrault And Francois: They are men of the North who depend upon dogs for survival. Later they play an important part in Buck's life.

Spitzenbergen: The dog who tried to steal Buck's food. He has been in the North before. As the story progresses, he becomes a very important part of it.

Curly: A somewhat happy-go-lucky Newfoundland dog. She plays a more important part in Chapter II.

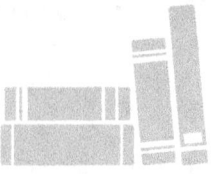

CALL OF THE WILD

TEXTUAL ANALYSIS

CHAPTER II

In Chapter I, Buck learned the law of the club; that is he learned that he was no match for a man with a club. In Chapter II, Buck learns the law of the fang; that is the fact that in the wilderness the laws of civilization, man-made laws, do not exist. Each individual, whether animal or man, is on his own to survive as best he can. Every other individual is at least a potential enemy, if not an actual enemy. Only the fittest and strongest will survive.

We can enumerate six incidents in this chapter by which we can trace Buck's progression, or rather retrogression*, toward the complete primeval animal. At the beginning of the chapter, Buck is the uninitiated civilized dog from the warm Southland. At the end of it, the domesticated generations have fallen away from him. He has lost the traces of civilization which it had taken

---
* retrogression-a going back

centuries to develop. In simple language, he was again the wild animal that his ancestors had been.

The first of the six incidents related is the fight between Curly and the husky dog. Curly, like Buck, was from the South and was used to a friendly existence. When she made her advances to the husky, she did not expect to be attacked so viciously in return. Also, Curly was not used to the wolf manner of fighting-to strike and then to run away. However, as far as Buck was concerned, the horrible part of the whole affair was the way in which the other dogs crowded around the combatants, ready to attack the loser. After these other dogs had been beaten off by Perrault, Francois and their friends, Buck could see that Curly had been torn to shreds. From this fight Buck learned that important lesson that only the winner has friends. The loser is everybody's enemy and fair game for all.

The second incident relates Buck's first experience with the harness which was put on him by Francois. Buck was then put between Spitz, the lead dog, and Dave. Although he resented being made a draft animal, Buck did not dare to disobey the stern Francois who never hesitated to use the whip. He soon learned to go at "mush," to stop at "ho," and to swing wide at the bends of the trail.

The third incident starts with the procuring by Perrault of three new dogs. Two, Billee and Joe, were brothers, but as different in temperament as day and night. Spitz, the leader of the pack, was able to bully the friendly Billee, but he could do nothing with the vicious Joe. The third dog, Sol-leks, which means the Angry One, had a battle-scarred face and but one eye. From Sol-leks Buck learned a lesson, and that was not to bother any dog that showed he wanted to be left alone. When Buck approached Sol-leks on his blind side, the dog whirled upon him and slashed his shoulder. Buck retreated, but later he became good friends with this dog.

The fourth incident relates how Buck learned to protect himself from the night cold. When, attracted by its warmth, Buck went into the tent of Francois and Perrault to sleep that first night, he was driven out by the two men. Then he lay down on the snow, but the frost soon drove him to his feet. Wandering about in search of some warm sleeping place, he was continually chased. Finally the thought struck him that he should try to find his teammates who had mysteriously disappeared. Roaming about aimlessly, Buck felt the snow suddenly give way beneath his forelegs. In he toppled upon the friendly Billee, and thus learned the secret of how the dogs of the Northland protected themselves against the cold. Buck then went and dug himself his own hole in the snow where he could get a warm, though fitful, night's rest.

The next morning the overland trip began, and Buck was assigned the place in front of Dave, the wheeler or sled dog. Sol-leks was given the position in front of Buck, for it was up to him and Dave to teach Buck the art of pulling a sled over the ice-covered trails. Gradually, though with some difficulty, Buck learned to do what was required of him.

Perhaps Buck's greatest problem was his hunger. He never seemed to be able to get his fill of food, and this leads us to the sixth incident of the chapter, that of the theft. Buck learned things easily, so when he saw Pike, one of the other dogs, steal some bacon from Perrault, he decided to try the same thing himself. This he did the next day and was successful at it, for Dub, another dog, was punished for Buck's misdeed.

Comment

The incident of the theft marked Buck as fit to survive in the Northland because it marked the end of his code of morality. The only important law was that of survival, and Buck had learned that the only way to survive was to rely on one's own ability to outwit everyone else.

It is in the last few paragraphs of Chapter II that Jack London makes his commentary on life. In the Southland, that is, in civilization, private property and personal feelings are important. However, in the Northland, that is, away from civilization, these things do not matter one bit. Survival is what counts, and the only person who will survive is the one who can adapt, the one who can strip away the **conventions** of civilization. The law of the club and the fang is the only law that prevails.

In the last short paragraph of Chapter II, London sums up the whole idea. Why was Buck forced to return to nature? It is first of all because man found gold in the North. It is secondly, and more importantly, because civilization did not take care of its own needs. Manuel, the gardener's helper, did not receive wages that would enable him to take care of his wife and children. Thus he was moved by necessity to kidnap Buck and to sell him. This is London's short socialistic commentary on life. If civilization, as represented by Judge Miller, paid Manuel his living wage, then Buck would not have been forced into the primitive struggle for existence. Thus man's selfishness and greed drive him back to his primitive animal instincts.

Character Analysis

Buck: In this chapter Buck is transformed. From the civilized dog at the beginning of the chapter, he becomes the complete animal at the end.

Curly: Another dog who, like Buck, is from the South. She is destroyed because she is not able to cope with the viciousness of the Northern husky.

Spitz: This is the dog that tried to steal from Buck's food. In this chapter we see him as being vicious, for he is among the dogs who await the defeat of Curly. He is, however, also the leader of the team.

Sol-leks: He is a dog who has faced the trials of the North and has survived. His name means the Angry One. He has learned not to trust anyone. Though he is a good team dog, he does not let Spitz bully him.

Billee, Joe, Dave, Pike, and Dub: These are the other dogs on the team.

Perrault And Francois: These two are yet to play their real part in Buck's story.

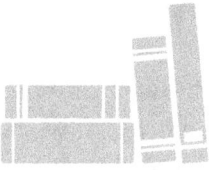

CALL OF THE WILD

TEXTUAL ANALYSIS

CHAPTER III

Chapter III brings to the foreground the struggle between Buck and Spitz which had been seething since the two dogs first came together on the Narwhal. During that first meal together, it was Spitz who stole from Buck's food. During the fight in which Curly was killed, it was Spitz who had stood on the edge of the crowd of dogs, licking his lips and waiting for the kill. Lastly, it was Spitz who was the leader of the team, and who, as leader, forced Buck to pull his share of the load. Remember that on Judge Miller's estate Buck had been king, subject to no one. Only with difficulty had he learned the law of the club and the fang. However, now that he had learned it, it was strong in him. Also the urge for his old supremacy was returning.

The first outbreak of trouble between Buck and Spitz occurred early in the trip. Driving snow, wind, and darkness had forced Francois and Perrault to select a camping site that was little to their liking. Behind them was a wall of rock, and the camp itself was actually on the frozen lake. Buck dug himself a sleeping place which he was unwilling to leave even to eat. When he returned from eating, however, there was Spitz in his nest. The beast in Buck roared, and he sprang at the other dog with a fury that surprised them both. A fight would have ensued if it had not been for an unexpected event which occurred at that moment-the camp was invaded by a horde of starving wild dogs.

Drawn by the smell of food, four or five score of hunger-crazed dogs swooped down upon the camp. There was no repelling them, for their hunger made them fearless. When Francois saw one of the dogs with his head in the grub box, he hit it with his club so hard that the box spilled all over the ground. The dogs then could not be beaten off until all this food was gone.

In the meantime the team had burst out of their nests to attack the invaders, but they themselves were driven back. When Francois and Perrault came to help the team, the wild dogs rushed back to the grub box. Thus the two men were busy chasing the savage beasts from one side of the camp to the other. Finally, the team dogs ran away into the woods, and the two men were eventually able to drive out the invaders.

Later in the night, the team gathered in the forest and sought shelter. They had not been pursued, but they were all badly chewed by the marauders. Joe had lost an eye, and Billee had had an ear chewed to ribbons. The danger to each was that he might be maddened by the many bites that he had received at the hands of the savage dogs.

The next morning, when the team returned to the camp, they found it a shambles. The invaders had chewed everything that was the least bit eatable-sled lashings, canvas covers. Perrault's moccasins, etc. It was two hours of hard work before the men had everything in shape so that they could move on.

Comment

The importance of this incident in the novel is two-fold. First, by it the author shows the savage fury of the wild dogs when driven by hunger. More important, though, he shows the really treacherous nature of Spitz. While the team dogs are fighting off the invaders, Spitz attacks Buck twice. The first time is when Buck is fighting another dog, and Spitz attacks him from the side. The second time, Spitz rushes at Buck to try to push him under the legs of the onrushing horde of dogs. Fortunately, Buck saves himself in both incidents. However, the author brings out by these two attacks the fact that the real struggle is that between Buck, the dog of the Southland, and Spitz, the dog of the Northland.

It took the group six days to cross the dangerous Thirty Mile River. Perrault had to lead the way across the treacherous ice. A dozen times it broke under him. Whenever this happened, it was necessary to stop and build a fire. The temperature was fifty below zero; so if Perrault did not dry out as quickly as possible, he would freeze to death. Once the sled broke through with Dave and Buck. The usual fire was needed for them. Another time Spitz and all the dogs up to Buck went through the ice, necessitating another fire. All these things delayed them greatly on their journey.

By the time the group made the Hootalinqua, Buck was played out. Remember he was not born to the North as the other dogs were. Therefore, every night Francois would rub his feet for half an hour. The man even sacrificed the tops of his moccasins to make four little ones for Buck's tender feet.

One morning the unexpected happened. The dog Dolly went suddenly mad and began to chase Buck. After a long run and much circling around, Buck was finally able to run by Francois so that he could smash Dolly with the ax and kill her. Here, however, is where the real treachery of Spitz again showed itself, for he attacked the exhausted Buck. But Francois was there with his whip to beat him off. Open warfare broke out between the two dogs. From this point on, Buck constantly challenged the leadership of Spitz. He would himself refuse to obey and would spring to the defense of the other dogs when they refused to obey the leader. This situation continued until the group reached their destination, Dawson.

Comment

This struggle between Buck and Spitz is important for two reasons. First of all, in order for the team to be successful, the dogs must work as a unit behind one leader. Mutiny, especially in fifty below temperature and with life and limb constantly in danger, is the worst possible thing that could happen. Even the madness of Dolly is not so bad a problem as this.

The second reason for the importance of this struggle is that in reality it is not one between two dogs. It is the struggle between the civilization of the South and the primitiveness of the North. Buck is the civilized South, unused to primitive conditions. Spitz is the beast of the North. The question is: Which one will survive, and by what means?

Buck found in Dawson what he had found everywhere else in the North-men working day and night, and dogs doing the work which the horses in the Southland did. Although there were a few dogs like Buck, who were from the South, most of them were of the wild wolf husky breed. Regularly every night they would set to howling, and Buck would join in this primitive song that would carry him back through the ages to the time of his wild fathers.

After seven days in Dawson, the return trip began. Perrault, carrying urgent dispatches, determined to make record time. He was able to travel light because the trail, which they had broken on the way in, was now packed down by later journeyers; and also, the police had deposits of grub arranged in two or three places along the way. Buck, however, in his continuing dispute with Spitz, had caused dissention within the ranks of the dogs, who needed a strong leader. When the team saw the authority of the lead dog so openly threatened by Buck, they also refused to follow. Worse yet, they began to complain and to bicker among themselves. The dispute between Spitz and Buck had to be settled, and the sooner the better.

One night after supper, the dog Dub turned up a snowshoe rabbit, but missed getting it. The chase began with Buck leading the pack. Spitz, however, instead of following the crowd, cut across a narrow neck of land, got in front of the rabbit, cut off his path, and killed him. Driven by the death-chase and hungry for blood, Buck crashed in upon Spitz, and the battle was on. Spitz, the experienced fighter, had much the better of it over the inexperienced Buck, who fought only by instinct. Every time that Buck rushed, he was slashed and driven off by the other dog. He was winded and almost defeated when suddenly he got an idea. On his next rush, Buck pretended that he was going for the throat of Spitz, but instead turned and bit hard into his foreleg, breaking it. Repeating the same trick, Buck then broke the other foreleg of Spitz, leaving him now completely helpless. It was time for the kill, and Buck lost little time with it.

Comment

Note that in this **episode** London spends little time describing the chase itself. On the other hand, he describes the mood of Buck. It is the urge to kill, the beast-instinct that drives Buck on after the rabbit. Surging up within him, this urge drives Buck forward. When he sees Spitz in front of him, killing the rabbit, Buck is then carried away by this killer-urge so that he attacks Spitz. The beast-instinct to kill is aroused in Buck by the snowshoe rabbit. When he is outsmarted by Spitz in his attack upon it, he turns this killer-instinct automatically upon the other dog. After all, Spitz had been his real enemy from the beginning.

What does the death of Spitz do to Buck? It completes the change in him. The civilized dog from the South has conquered the uncivilized dog from the North, but what has it done to him? This victory is the last thing necessary to transform Buck. He has tasted the blood of his own kind. He is now the primordial* beast.

Character Analysis

Buck: In this chapter Buck develops completely. He has learned the law of the club and the fang. Here he puts them to use to kill his one last enemy.

Spitz: This is a dog which is vicious by nature. He shows his meanness by attacking Buck when he least expects it; that is, when Buck is tired or doing something else. He is defeated because he uses only his savage ability, whereas Buck uses his head and thereby tricks him.

---

* primordial-primitive or primeval

Perrault And Francois: These men are more important in this chapter. Twice Francois saves Buck's life-once from Dolly, and once from Spitz.

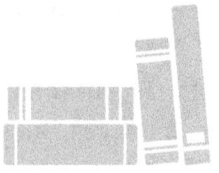

CALL OF THE WILD

TEXTUAL ANALYSIS

CHAPTER IV

Buck had defeated Spitz, his arch-enemy. Therefore, he concluded, he should now be the leader of the team. Francois and Perrault, however, had other ideas. They selected Sol-leks, the older and more experienced dog, as the leader. Buck would not hear of this and refused to allow himself to be harnessed in his usual position in front of Dave. For almost an hour the two men chased Buck around the camp, but the dog would not yield. Finally the men had to give in, and Buck was given the position at the head of the team.

Comment

In this section of the story, note how Buck outwits the two men with clubs. He had conquered the law of the fang by using trickery to defeat Spitz. Here he conquers against the club. Buck now knows how to keep out of its range and how to dodge it. He no longer charges, as he did against the man in the red sweater, but waits and finally wins.

Francois and Perrault had both fore valued Buck highly. However, as highly as they had thought of him before, they saw now, when he took up the leadership, that they had really undervalued him. Buck turned out to be an even greater leader than Spitz. This was shown in the way Buck restored unity to the team. He forced Pike to pull more than his share of the load; and he punished Joe, the sour one. Spitz had never been able to do either of these things. Thus the men were able to bring the mail into Skagway in the record time of fourteen days, an average of forty miles a day. The team and the men were the center of admiration. However, after all the excitement was over, Perrault and Francois received official orders that the team was to be turned over to a Scotch half-breed as part of a new mail train. The two men were to pass out of Buck's life forever.

Comment

Note the casual way in which the author takes Francois and Perrault out of the story. With just a sentence or two they are gone. They've served their purpose in the narrative by breaking Buck into the life of the trail. Now they are no longer needed. London does, however, show the affection between man and dog when he says that Francois wept over leaving Buck.

Out on the trail again-this time with the Scotch half-breed-Buck found life very difficult and monotonous*. He was not now with a single team, but in company with a dozen others that made up the mail train. Frequently at night, when worn

---

* monotonous-boring, without variation

out from the day's heavy work, Buck would lie by the fire and dream. Sometimes the dream would be about Judge Miller's estate. More often it would be about the man in the red sweater or the fight with Spitz. Sometimes, though, Buck would have an unusual dream of fearsome beasts of prey and a strange man, with hairy body and ape-like stance, more animal than human; for Buck, in his dreams, was hearkening back to the days of his primitive ancestors.

Comment

Jack London's use of the dream in this section of the story is considered by many critics to be very poor. The author wants to show us that Buck is becoming more and more conscious of his beastly ancestors; but, for the modern reader especially, the description of the cave man tends to be more humorous than serious. It seems obviously copied from some science book on evolution that may have been popular during the author's day. The scientists of our times, even those who hold to the theory of evolution, do not put much store in the ape-like descriptions of ancient man. Thus in our day, this scene loses much of its effectiveness.

The last **episode** in Chapter IV is the story of Dave. The trip was hard on all the dogs because of the heavy loads and also because new snow made the trails perilous. However, Dave seemed to suffer most. He was the wheeler or sled dog; that is, he was the first dog in line after the sled. It was his job to keep the heavy load balanced. Something went wrong with him, and he became morose* and sullen. Realizing this, the men examined him to try to discover what his trouble was but could

---

* morose-fretful, gloomy

find nothing. When they tried to rest him by taking him out of the traces, Dave resented it and refused to run free behind the sled. On one occasion he bit through the traces in order to try to get back into line. Seeing his anxiety, the men put Dave back with the team, but he was too weak to pull his load. There was nothing that the men could do except to mercifully put him out of his misery. This they did.

Comment

No lover of dogs can help but be impressed by the sympathetic way in which London tells the story of Dave. Here is a dog born and bred to the harness. He wants nothing more than to die in it. The men want to allow him this, but it is too much for him. He merely suffers more, and they must shoot him. However, the author makes no cynical* remark about ending a useless life. The dog must die rather than suffer. As the story progresses, you will see that London does not always treat his humans so kindly.

Character Analysis

Buck: In this chapter he becomes the leader. He has learned the law of the club and the fang, and he uses them for his own advantage.

    Perrault And Francois: These men appear in the story for the last time. We see their attachment to the dogs when Francois weeps in saying good-bye to Buck.

---

* cynical-pessimistic, sneering

Dave: The sled dog captures the reader's attention and sympathy. In a sad way, he is the hero of the last part of the story; for we admire his desire to stay in the traces and to work until death at the job which had been his whole life.

CALL OF THE WILD

TEXTUAL ANALYSIS

CHAPTER V

The work of pulling the heavy mail sleds over the icy trails was indeed difficult. When the sleds pulled into Skagway after a thirty-day haul from Dawson, the dogs were footsore and completely worn out. In less than five months this team had covered more than twenty-five hundred miles. The drivers too were trail-weary and expected to rest. The men had to go out again, but the dogs were too tired and too weak for another trip. Therefore, they had to be sold.

The scene for Buck's next adventure is set very rapidly. We are told that the dogs are tired; but it is the description of the two men who buy them, and then that of the woman, which forewarns us of the difficulties to come. Charles is middle-aged and has weak and watery eyes. Hal is young and showy. He carries a big Colt revolver and a hunting knife strapped around him. Mercedes is his sister and Charles' wife. They are from the South and are used to the comforts of civilization. They've brought unnecessary articles with them, such as dishes, a tent, and too many clothes. What is worse, the two men don't know how to pack the gear so that it will balance well on the sled. As a result, the group becomes the object of the ridicule of the bystanders.

When the dogs can't move the sleds, Hal becomes enraged and begins to whip them. To add to the confusion, Mercedes, moved with womanly pity, interferes to stop her brother from beating the dogs. This further enrages Hal. One of the onlookers, for the sake of the dogs, tells Hal to break loose the runners of the sled which were frozen fast. This Hal does and the dogs struggle frantically ahead. A short distance on, the path turned and sloped steeply. As the dogs made the turn, the sled went over, spilling half the load through the loose lashings. Freed from the excessive weight, the dogs raced forward. Paying no attention to the calls of Hal, they ran on their way, picking up speed as the rest of the gear spilled off the sled.

Comment

In the first four chapters, we saw a dog taken from civilization and exposed to the ravages* of the North. We also saw how this dog learned to survive in the fight against nature. This dog Buck is now a part of the North. In Chapter V, we see the author, in a sense, backtrack. He now brings in three people from the Southland and exposes them to the ravages of the North. Buck, as leader of the team, is responsible, so to speak, for their survival. We have seen the first inability of these people. As the story progresses, we will see how they do in their struggle against nature.

With the help of some kindhearted citizens, the dogs were caught and returned to their owners. The people of Skagway gave some advice to the outsiders, telling them to get rid of

---

* ravage-ruin, damage

all their unnecessary supplies. Even with this, the outfit was still quite heavy, so Hal and Charles bought six Outside dogs, which made fourteen in all. The two men had everything figured mathematically, but they had overlooked one small detail: the fact that one sled could not carry enough food for fourteen dogs.

Late the next morning, Buck led the long team up the street toward the trail. There was nothing snappy about them, for the old dogs were tired and the new dogs frightened. Buck seemed to sense that these humans could not be relied upon because they did not know how to do anything. It took them half the night to pitch a slovenly* camp, and half the morning to pack. The trip was a miserable one for both dogs and man. When the dogs did not go fast enough, the men beat them or overfed them. When the food began to run short, the men underfed the dogs. One thing led to another. The three humans argued constantly. The dogs weakened and died one by one until finally only five of them remained. Both man and dog were in a pitiable condition when they staggered into John Thornton's camp at the mouth of White River.

Comment

Note that in this **episode** it is spring, the time when the sun rises earlier each day and sets later. New life-plant and animal- was bursting out all over. The earth was trying to break loose from the sheet of ice that had held it prisoner all winter. In sorry contrast to this scene of new life were Hal, Charles and Mercedes. While nature was coming to life, they were dying; for the simple reason that they did not know how to contend with nature. They had brought with them from the Southland all

---
* slovenly-carelessly or lazily

the comforts of civilization. But these comforts did not belong in the uncivilized North. They only made the sled heavier, the travel slower. The three humans had also brought the ideas of the Southland with them into the North. Mercedes, for example, thought that she should receive the same gentle treatment that a lady in civilization deserves. But there was neither time nor place for chivalry in the uncivilized North, and her insistence on riding on the sled only made matters worse. In other words, these three people were finding themselves unfit in the struggle against nature.

When the group staggered into John Thornton's camp, both man and dog were exhausted. Thornton, the experienced man of the North, paid little attention to Hal when he boasted of how his group had succeeded in spite of all the warnings they had received. Thornton knew it was useless to try to talk to people such as they were. However, when the group wanted to move along, Thornton saw that the dogs would not at first get up. Buck especially would not move, even under the beating that Hal was giving him. His animal instinct gave him a warning of the danger close at hand. The ice under his feet had been thin and rotting, not firm enough to be trusted. Also he cared little about whether or not the group moved on. John Thornton, however, angered by the merciless stupidity of Hal, got between him and Buck. After knocking Hal's knife from his hand, John Thornton picked it up and cut Buck loose from the sled. The three Outside people really had no fight left in them, and gave up Buck as too near dead to be useful. They were willing enough just to be on their way. However, they should have followed the advice of the men of the North, for about a quarter of a mile down the trail, the ice gave way beneath them. The bottom dropped out of the trail and in a few seconds sled, dogs and humans disappeared.

Comment

Note the contempt with which Jack London treats these three people from civilization. They are, for example, fools who cannot be separated from their folly*. When they plunge to their death, John Thornton utters no word of sympathy for them. Instead all of his sympathy is turned towards the dog Buck.

What is the meaning of this chapter? As we pointed out before, the first four chapters show us how a civilized dog is brought to the Northland, and how by instinct he learns to survive. This chapter now brings three civilized humans to the Northland. They are supposed to have intelligence, to be able to reason things out. However, this does not help them to survive. They do not use it to learn from other humans as Buck had learned from the other dogs. They rely rather on notions which they had obtained in the civilized South. As a result, they do not conquer nature. Instead, they are gobbled up by it. In other words, the dog is better equipped to survive against the forces of nature than are these people. Buck's animal instinct helps him to adapt himself to the struggle. Their human nature leads them into being quarrelsome and boastful failures.

Character Analysis

Buck: In this chapter Buck plays little active part. He is the dog leader of the team. His main importance is as a contrast to the humans.

---

* folly-foolishness

Charles: A weak character, he stays in the background while Hal does all the talking.

Hal: A boastful young man, he will not listen to anyone. He thinks that his big Colt revolver and his hunting knife are the signs of a strong man. He learns, however, that they will not help him fight the cold and hunger of the North.

Mercedes: A woman who expects to find soft treatment in the North, she finds instead only cold and hunger. Nature, in its harsh dealings with mankind, does not make any distinctions between male and female. Only the hardy will survive.

John Thornton: A man who has learned to live with nature, he knows that it is foolish to travel when the spring thaws are in progress. He shows great sympathy for Buck, but very little for the three people.

CALL OF THE WILD

TEXTUAL ANALYSIS

CHAPTER VI

....

While Chapter V showed us the inability of some men to survive in the North because of their unwillingness to adapt themselves to it, Chapter VI shows us how man and dog, working together, are able to overcome great difficulties. When John Thornton rescued Buck from the three Outsiders, he had been recovering from a case of frozen feet. His partners had made him comfortable and left him the previous December to recover, while they went up river to get out a raft of logs for Dawson. Under the care of this man, Buck gradually won back his strength.

With Thornton there were two dogs, Skeet and Nig. Skeet was an Irish setter who took upon herself the task of looking after Buck. Nig was a huge black dog who proved to be equally friendly. With these three, the man and the two other dogs, Buck learned the meaning of real love. Even at Judge Miller's place, this love had not existed. There Buck was at best a companion. Here, not only had John Thornton saved Buck's life, but he had also made himself a real friend. Thornton was the kind of man who took care of his dogs as though they were his own children.

And Buck returned this affection. His experience thus far in the North had taught him that no master could be permanent. Thus, through love of this man, as well as through fear of losing him, Buck followed John Thornton wherever he went from morning until night. Even at night, the dog would sometimes creep to the flap of the tent, listen for the man's breathing, and then lie there.

Buck was not, however, returning to the ways of civilization. He had learned the law of the club and the fang too well. Although he would not fight with either Skeet or Nig, he was the merciless foe of any strange dog that dared come near the camp. It was only his love for John Thornton that really kept him where he was. Buck sat by this man's feet night after night, eating, drinking, scenting the wind, and listening to the sounds of the forest. When Buck would lie down to sleep at night, the shades of his past and the sounds of the wild forest would beckon him. More and more this dog lost his interest in humanity and in civilization. Oftentimes he would run off into the forest, only to return at the thought of John Thornton.

Comment

In the first few pages of this chapter, the author shows us the picture of an animal-the dog Buck-who is caught in the struggle between civilization and the "call of the wild." For Buck, John Thornton represents not just civilization, but a kind of the perfection of the love which should exist between creatures. John is now Buck's sole tie with the civilized world. Buck has learned that nothing really lasts. His comfortable life at Judge Miller's estate was snatched away from him. Each of his masters disappeared from his life just as quickly. In the meantime, Buck was learning the cruel, hard facts of life-the law of the club and the fang. For Buck life is a matter of killing or being killed. The urge to return to the life of his ancestors is strong in him. However, each time he wanders off into the forest, the thought of John Thornton calls him back.

The rest of this chapter narrates four incidents which demonstrate the complete devotion of the dog Buck to the man John Thornton. The first of these took place while John and his two partners were sitting on the edge of a cliff. John, on a thoughtless whim to prove Buck's loyalty, ordered him to jump. Before Thornton knew what was happening, Buck was almost over the cliff. It took all his strength, plus that of his two partners, to pull the dog back.

The second incident took place at Circle City. Black Burton, an ill-tempered man, was picking a quarrel with a tenderfoot. When Thornton stepped in to stop the quarrel, Burton struck out and sent him sprawling. Before anyone knew what had happened, Buck was upon the man. Burton saved himself only by instinctively throwing up his arm. Even so, a second later, Buck was at his throat. It took the crowd to drive the dog off. Later a "miners' meeting" cleared Buck of any charges, but his reputation was made.

The third incident was in the fall of the same year. The three partners were lining a poling boat down the rapids. Hans and Pete were on the shore, guiding the boat with ropes, while Thornton was in it. When Hans checked the boat too suddenly with his end of the rope, it overturned, flinging Thornton out. He was carried downstream toward the worst part of the rapids, where no swimmer could expect to survive. Buck sprang into the water instantly and reached Thornton. When he felt John grasp him, Buck headed slowly for shore. However, they could not make it, and Thornton yelled for him to go. Buck swam back to shore while Thornton clung to a rock. Hans and Pete attached a rope to Buck who tried twice to swim out to his master and was finally successful in reaching him. John Thornton wrapped his arms around the dog, and the two men on shore pulled them in. This heroic action further endeared Buck to him.

That winter at Dawson was the scene of the fourth incident. John Thornton got involved in a bragger's argument and bet that Buck could start a load of one thousand pounds, something unheard of. The bet was for a thousand dollars which neither John nor his two partners had. However, a friend, Jim O'Brien, was able to lend it to him.

As part of the bet, it was agreed that Buck would have to break the runners of the sled loose from the frozen grip of the snow. The team of ten dogs was unhitched, and Buck alone was harnessed to the sled. The excitement of the crowd mounted, and even Buck seemed to become more eager. John Thornton knelt beside him and whispered the words, "As you love me, Buck. As you love me." Buck grabbed the man's hand between his teeth as if in answer. Then, following Thornton's orders to gee and to haw and to mush*, Buck used every ounce of his energy to break the sled loose, to start it moving, and finally to pull it the one hundred yards which had been agreed upon. Hands and mittens went into the air as great cheers arose for the dog and his accomplishment. Thornton, however, merely fell on his knees by the dog and rose weeping.

Comment

In this chapter the author shows the cooperation that can exist between man and beast. If the man is one who loves and

---

* to haw, to gee, to mush-words of command to animals to go to the left, to the right, or straight ahead

respects the animal, the animal will return this love and respect a hundredfold. The dog does not have to become a part of wild nature. If he has an attachment to civilization, as Buck had to John Thornton, he will remain a part of it.

Character Analysis

Buck: In this chapter Buck is a dog who has only one friend, John Thornton. He proves his love for this man by the things he does for him.

John Thornton: This is a man full of kindness. He is not afraid of the wild, and approaches it, as he does everything else, with kindness and love.

Skeet And Nig: These are two dogs who help draw a contrast with those who appeared earlier in the story. Even though they are exposed to the ravages of the North, they keep their friendly ways. This is, of course, because they are treated with love by John Thornton.

Hans And Pete: The two partners of John Thornton have no real character of their own. They are in the story simply because they are needed to perform actions such as pull John and Buck out of the water.

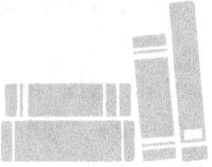

CALL OF THE WILD

TEXTUAL ANALYSIS

CHAPTER VII

In this chapter our story is completed. Thus far we have seen Buck transformed from a civilized dog into one perfectly able to live by the law of the club and the fang. We have seen him almost die as the result of the ignorance of the three Outsiders, Charles, Hal, and Mercedes. Then we have seen him cling to civilization in the person of John Thornton. Finally, now, in this chapter we will see him answer the "call of the wild."

With the thousand dollars that Buck had won for John Thornton, plus an extra six thousand which was made on a side bet, the three partners-John, Hans, and Pete-were able to pay off their debts and then to journey into the East to find a fabled* lost gold mine. Many men had sought this mine; few had found it; and many more had never returned from their search for it. This lost mine was shrouded in mystery. Dying men had sworn to its existence and to that of the cabin which was supposed to mark

---

* fabled-like a fable, legendary

its site. However, no one knew its location for sure. Thornton Hans, and Pete, therefore, were facing an unknown trail when they moved off toward the East in search of success where others had found only failure.

Comment

The author creates an air of mystery in the beginning of this chapter. The idea of a lost gold mine, a deserted cabin, nuggets unlike any known in the Northland, all provide the reader with a sense of suspense and of curiosity about the future of the characters.

Also in this chapter the reader gets a fuller picture of John Thornton as the link between civilization and the wild. He asked little of either one. He could live in the one or the other. With only the barest necessities, he could plunge into the wilderness and could survive wherever he pleased and for as long as he pleased.

On this trip the men were traveling Indian-fashion, hunting their food as they went along and also moving slowly. To Buck this journey was a boundless pleasure. There wasn't the pressure of the earlier mail runs he had made with Francois and Perrault. This group he was with now would travel for a few weeks and then camp for a few weeks. Time passed. Winter turned into summer, and then came back again. Spring came on once more and the group found not the lost cabin, but a broad valley where each day's work earned them thousands of dollars in clean gold dust and nuggets.

While the men worked panning their gold, there was little for the dogs to do save occasionally haul in some freshly killed meat. Buck had more time for leisure; and as he lay by the fire, the vision of his hairy cave man would come back to him. In these dreams of the ancient times, the most outstanding element seemed to be fear. The man in Buck's dreams appeared to be frightened of his surroundings and to be ever on the alert for trouble.

Comment

To some extent in this section of the story, London is able to bring out the joys of life in the open, with its hunting, fishing, and adventure. Unfortunately, however, he again brings into the story the hairy cave man. This is supposed to be a symbol of Buck's wild past calling him back to uncivilized life. As we pointed out earlier, this picture of the evolutionary man does not appeal to the educated mind of our times. Consequently, it tends to spoil the story for us.

Unlike the segment about the cave man, however, the description of Buck's urge to run through the forest is interesting and appealing. Irresistible urges would suddenly come upon him as he lay sleeping by the fire. He would cock his ears, listen, spring up, and then dash through the forest for hours at a time. He was in search of that one thing that seemed to be calling him into the wild. His primitive instincts were becoming sharper.

One night Buck awoke with a start. He heard a strange call from the forest that was distinct and definite. It was a long-drawn howl unlike any made by a husky dog. He sprang through the sleeping camp and into the woods where he came upon a lean timber wolf. Buck approached the wolf in a half-friendly, half-threatening manner. However, the other animal turned and ran away. When he had run as far as he could, the wolf turned on

Buck and was prepared to fight. Buck, however, did not attack but made friendly advances. The wolf again ran away and Buck again chased him. This was repeated a few times until the wolf finally realized that Buck's intentions were friendly. Then he returned the friendship, rubbed noses with him, and began to play with him. After a while the wolf loped away and Buck followed. Together they ran through the woods as brothers, so to speak. Buck was answering the first real "call of the wild."

After running freely through the forest for several hours, the two animals stopped for a drink of water. When they did, Buck remembered John Thornton. With this he turned around and began to head for the camp. The wolf followed for a while trying to persuade Buck to come back with him, but the dog would not. He ran away from the other animal who set up a mournful howl for him. Buck, however, returned to the camp where he found John Thornton eating dinner. For two days and two nights, he never left the camp, never let the man out of his sight. In spite of his association with the timber wolf, he was still attached to civilization in the person of this man Thornton.

Comment

The wolf howl is a part of the "call of the wild." The wolf is a breed of uncivilized dog, and Buck is attracted to this wood brother. He has learned to love the free and easy life of being able to run about at will. However, he is still attached to civilization as represented by John Thornton. This is the only creature whom Buck ever really loved and was loved by in return. Therefore, he was not yet prepared to desert civilization forever.

Buck, however, began to stay away from the camp for days, not even returning to sleep. He fished for salmon in a broad stream, and on one occasion killed a large black bear that had been blinded by the mosquitoes. After this, the blood longing became stronger. Buck became more self-reliant. Except for a little brown and white in his coloring, he might have been mistaken for a giant wolf. His St. Bernard father had given him size and weight. His shepherd mother had given him a beautiful shape. Both parents contributed to his intelligence. His cunning was a wolf-like cunning. He was now in peak condition, vigorous and alert. He had all the qualities that led John Thornton to say, "Never was there such a dog."

When Buck marched out of camp, a transformation came over him. He was no longer the playful friend of John Thornton, but a wild animal who lived solely by his own skills. He used all the trickery of the forest to trap and kill his own food. He did not, however, kill simply for the pleasure of it, but only for food. When he was not hungry, he would practice his skills by trapping animals and then letting them escape.

In the fall of the year the moose appeared in greater abundance. They were heading for their winter quarters. One day Buck, while looking for new quarry, came upon a herd of twenty which was led by a great bull. Buck decided to go after the leader because, although he was savage in appearance, he was also wounded. A feathered arrow end stuck out from his side. Buck used all his trickery to separate the bull from the herd; but each time he thought he succeeded, some of the younger bulls would come to the rescue of their leader. However, after a while the younger ones gave up their protection of the wounded old one. It was, after all, only his life that was really at stake. Their job was to get down to the valleys so that they could get protection for the winter.

Once the old bull was on his own, it was simply a matter of time before the dog would have him. Buck's plan was to stalk his prey and to keep him away from food and water. At the end of the fourth day, his victory came. The moose did not have any energy left, and so the huge animal was conquered by the smaller, persistent one.

Comment

The descriptions in this chapter of Buck's run with the timber wolf and of his stalking the old bull moose have for their purpose to prepare the reader for the conclusion of the story. Not only has Buck now learned everything he need know in order to survive in the wilds of the forest, but he has actually survived on his own and conquered his enemies. The story is complete except for one last thing. John Thornton, Buck's only link to the civilized world, must be removed from the plot.

In this section of the story, the reader should also note the way in which the author tells of the desertion of the old bull moose by his younger followers. London treats this action as though it were to be expected. In other words, he is saying that one old life is not important. The lives of the young and strong are the only thing that matter. This he does in order to emphasize his **theme** that only the strong survive. As Hal, Charles, and Mercedes plunged to their death because they were unfit to survive in the North, so the old bull moose is left to the mercy of Buck because he is no longer fit to survive.

After Buck had spent a day and a night eating and enjoying the moose, his greatest kill thus far, he once again turned back toward camp and John Thornton. A few times during the return journey he hesitated, but each time he decided to go on. Finally, when he reached a spot about three miles from the camp, he found a fresh trail which sent his neck hair rippling and bristling. Then he slid cautiously through the forest to the camp which he found in a shambles. Yeehats, northern Indians, were dancing about and celebrating. With ferocity, Buck attacked the group, leaping from one to the other and tearing each one apart. So great a fear did he create that the Yeehats fled in terror. They claimed they had seen the coming of the Evil Spirit. Buck pursued them for a while. Then he returned to camp where he found the dead body of John Thornton.

Comment

Note the savagery with which the author describes this scene of dog killing man. The men are the ones who become confused. So panic-stricken are they that they shoot each other in their attempt to kill Buck. The dog is the conqueror. His friend John Thornton is dead, but Buck has learned another new lesson. He can kill men. He need no longer be afraid of them unless they are carrying their arrows, spears, or clubs.

That night there was a full moon. With the coming of the night, Buck heard a stirring in the forest. Soon a pack of wolves moved into the camp. One bold one attacked Buck, but in a moment his neck was broken. Three more tried to get Buck, but each was conquered in his turn. Finally, the entire pack attacked Buck and drove him back into a bank from which he could not escape. However, they could not conquer him. Then Buck recognized the friendly timber wolf with whom he had run through the forest. After these two made friends again, an old wolf approached Buck in a friendly manner. Having realized that they could not conquer the big dog, they joined him.

Thus the story ends with Buck a member of the wolf pack. Soon after these last incidents, a new breed of wolves appeared on the scene. They had brown muzzles and white patches on their chests, and they were bigger than the usual wolf. These wolves spread terror throughout the country. Legends and rumors spread among the Yeehats, no one of whom would venture into that valley where John Thornton's camp had been. It was there that the Evil Spirit made his home.

Comment

Jack London makes much of the "call" or "calls of the wild." These are the sounds of the forest. The most important one is the howling of the wolf. Buck had been a civilized dog. He had gone through a series of experiences which taught him that only the strong survive. In this last chapter, Buck has made his two greatest conquests-that over man in the person of the Yeehats, and that over the animals by becoming the leader of the wolf pack. The plot is a success. Buck has heard the "call of the wild" and has answered it.

CHARACTER ANALYSIS AND THEME

Bucks Metamorphosis

In Chapter VII we see the completion of the metamorphosis in the character of Buck. This means that his character has changed completely. At the beginning of the story in Chapter I, Buck is a big, playful dog. He is the king of Judge Miller's estate, a king who goes where he wants and with whom he wants. He has no fear of anyone or anything because he has never had any reason to be afraid. Throughout Chapter II and Chapter III, however,

Buck learns that there are things to fear-men with clubs, other dogs, etc.-and that life is a struggle. He becomes sneaky and underhanded because these are qualities needed for survival. He becomes vicious in his struggles with the other dogs, especially those like Spitz, because where they are concerned he must either kill or be killed.

When John Thornton enters his life, Buck learns that it is possible to love and be loved in return. But it is Thornton who takes Buck out into the wilderness where he learns to hunt and to kill for food. Here Buck meets the wolf pack and once again he becomes a king. This time, however, he is not a playful companion. He is, instead, a vicious ruler. He leads his followers through the countryside, spreading terror, conquering, and killing. In other words, a playful, civilized dog has been changed into a vicious, wild wolf.

Bucks Last Hold On Civilization

John Thornton appears in Chapters VI and VII as a symbol of Buck's attachment to civilization. While this man is alive, the dog will not leave civilization entirely. But when Thornton dies, Buck goes off into the wild. There is, however, another point of interest which the author brings out in the character of John Thornton. In this novel the man provides a comparison for the dog. The author says that Thornton asks little either of civilization or of the wild. He is by nature playful, and he loves to roam through the forest in a free and easy manner. The only time he is ever known to be angry is when he sees Buck mistreated by the three Outsiders. He rises to the defense of the tenderfoot against the evil Black Burton, but the author does not say that he is angry. These same qualities-playfulness, friendliness, justice-exist in Buck. For example, he defends the weak when he fights for the members of the team that the evil Spitz is trying to bully.

Comparison Between Buck And Thornton

The reader might ask himself this question: Why does Buck survive and John Thornton die? The answer to this is very important because it contains the whole **theme** or idea of the story. Every human character in this novel disappears from the story rapidly and very often with little or no explanation. Manuel, the man in the red sweater, Perrault, Francois, Charles, Hal, Mercedes, all come and go. John Thornton is no exception. He is a human, and although he loves the wilderness, he perishes in it. Why? The answer is simply because he is a human with human weaknesses. It was greed for gold that led to Buck's kidnapping. It was greed for gold that caused the death of the three Outsiders. It was also greed for gold that brought John Thornton into the wilderness in search of the lost mine.

On the other hand, Buck is an animal. All he needs is food and some shelter. If he is stronger than the other animals, he can survive. He does, in fact, survive for that very reason. It is important for the reader to note that John Thornton is killed by other humans, the Yeehats. However, it is the dog who avenges his death. In other words, what Jack London is trying to say in this novel is that life is a struggle for all creatures. Man can survive, but he is not so well-equipped as the animal to do so. What is the reason for this? It is because man, even the best, like John Thornton, give in to greed and selfishness. They go after things that they do not really need for existence. On the other hand, the animal knows by instinct just what he needs and goes after that alone. For example, Buck, even when the blood longing became strong in him, killed only for food or to protect himself. He never killed for pleasure, because he was not greedy or selfish. His animal instincts led him to take from nature only what he needed for survival.

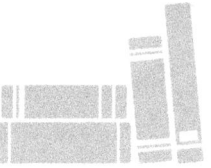

CALL OF THE WILD

ESSAY QUESTIONS AND ANSWERS

....

Question: What type of novel is *The Call of the Wild*?

Answer: *The Call of the Wild* is classified as a naturalistic novel. This means that the author tries to apply some scientific theory to the lives of his characters. In this novel, London is applying the theory of atavism. This means the theory that under certain circumstances a creature will revert to the characteristics of its ancestors. London takes the dog Buck out of his civilized environment and puts him into the wilderness. The idea behind this is to show that once the creature comforts of civilization are taken away from an individual and he is forced to fight for survival, he will become more and more like his barbaric ancestors. London is quite obvious in the way he goes about doing this. He makes direct use of such words as primordial and primitive. He repeatedly mentions Buck's ancestors recalling him to their ways of life. He twice has Buck dream of primitive times during which he sees a hairy cave man. Then, in the conclusion of the novel, Buck joins the wolf pack. It is London's **theme** that if our natural instincts are allowed to have free play, they will carry us back to the ways of our ancestors.

Question: What is the meaning of the short verse at the beginning of the novel?

Answer: In these few lines, London, the author, places before the reader the complete **theme** of his story. Throughout the entire first half of the story, London places the reader in Buck's position, as the dog is trained to the ways of the North country. Through this dangerous initiation, London stresses the theory "survival of the fittest" in such incidents that concern the "law of the club and the fang" and "kill or be killed." As the author keeps reminding the reader after every skirmish with the untame, after every lesson of nature, Buck learns not by experience alone. He also learns by instincts long dead which come alive again. The meaning behind those first four lines is just that. These old longings or instincts within Buck are yearning for "the call of the wild." However, they are somewhat hindered by custom's chain and by his soft life on the Judge's acres in the warm Santa Clara Valley. However, these hidden instincts are aroused from their long sleep when Buck realizes that to live he must put aside the ways of his docile nature. He must sharpen his keen animal instincts.

Question: Explain the reasons why Manuel kidnapped Buck?

Answer: There are three reasons for this action. They are as follows:

A. All stories must have an initial incident, and in this novel Manuel's action is this incident which starts the plot rolling. When Manuel kidnaps Buck, it begins the dog's adventuresome time in the North.

B. As far as the incident itself is concerned, Manuel was a gardener's helper on Judge Miller's estate. His salary was small, barely enough so that he and his family could get by.

However, Manuel was leading himself toward inevitable destruction through his love of a Chinese lottery. Moreover, he put his faith in a system, but this depended on money in abundance. His wages were insufficient, but he did find one solution. This rested upon Buck's worth in money to the thousands of gold seekers heading into the Northland. Unfortunately, in order to compensate for Manuel's sin, Buck would pay dearly.

C. The third reason concerns itself more directly with the **theme** of the novel. Manuel is a victim of society. If man, in the person of Judge Miller, had paid him a fair wage, Manuel would not have had to gamble in order to try to get money for his family.

Question: What is the general plot structure of this novel?

Answer: This novel is really a loosely constructed series of seven stories. The plot style is called episodic. This means that each part is a separate story in the life of the characters. All these **episodes** are connected by Buck, who is the only major character in the novel. The time element, since it is really not important to the **theme** of the story, is rather vague. The author mentions the seasons as coming and going, but he never mentions any special year. From the historical background of the novel, we know that the initial action must have been about 1896. This was the year of the start of the Alaskan gold rush. The action does move in an order of time, though. There is no use of such techniques as the flashback. Even the use of the dream technique does not destroy this time order of the action. Moreover, since London seems more intent on getting his idea across than on writing an obscure work, all the action is clear and to the point.

Question: Explain the law of the club and the law of the fang?

Answer: By the law of the club is meant that an animal is taught obedience to a man through the use of force. The animal is by nature a free creature. If man wants the animal to do his work for him, he must teach it not to respect himself personally. He must train it to respect and fear the pain that man can inflict upon it by beating. The animal does not obey through love but through fear.

By the law of the fang is meant that the animal must fight for survival. His struggle is against his fellow animals. The strong ones conquer the weak ones. The bigger ones use the smaller ones for food. In order to survive in the wilderness, the animal must use every talent it possesses. He must learn either to kill his enemies or to be killed by them. Only the fittest will survive.

Question: What are the major strengths and weaknesses of this novel?

Answer: The two major strengths of this novel are its freshness of romance and its reality of setting. By telling the story through the eyes of the dog Buck, Jack London takes the reader into a new world of adventure. The simplicity with which the story is told makes it very easy for the reader to put himself into it and to imagine that he is in the Northland. The reader can picture himself traveling across the frozen countryside. The exactness with which London describes a scene and mentions definite places, such as Dawson, give the story a reality. By naming lakes, rivers, and so forth-White Lake for example-the author establishes a certain authenticity to his story. In other words, the reader can easily put himself in the place of the dog Buck and can imagine himself being in such a place as Circle City in the great Northland.

The weakness lies perhaps in the lengths to which London will go to attempt to prove this theory of atavism. The rather heavy-handed passages in reference to the appearance of the primitive man in Buck's dreams are preposterous.

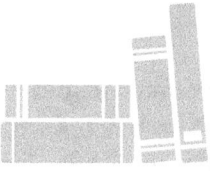

WHITE FANG

TEXTUAL ANALYSIS

CHAPTERS I–III

The introduction to the mood of this novel covers the first three chapters. Here the **theme** of the story is created by the desolateness of the setting. The author places the reader immediately in the frozen-hearted Northland Wild. It is here that we find two men who are returning to Fort McGurry with the dead body of a third man, Lord Alfred. The two men, Bill and Henry, are in real trouble since their supplies are very low. They have only three cartridges left. Besides this, the temperature has been fifty below zero for several days, and food has been very scarce. Each night, as they build their campfire, they can feel the eyes of the wolves staring at them. Their six dogs begin to disappear one at a time until there are only three remaining. The men know what is happening, but they cannot do anything about it.

Each night after dark, a she-wolf strayed into camp to lure one of the dogs away. Of course, as soon as the dog went out away from the protection of the camp, the wolf pack attacked and ate it. Both men become desperate, and Bill decides that he must get the she-wolf no matter what else happened. It was driving them insane with its tactics. However, since they had only three shells, he had to wait until he had a clear shot at the beast. The first time they saw the she-wolf in daylight, she was luring one of the dogs away from the sled. Bill tried to get a good shot at her, but his own dog was in the way. He couldn't take a chance on wasting a shot. Thus the wolf got away.

Bill, however took the rifle and went out after his tormentor. For a time Henry, who had stayed by the sled, heard nothing. Then there was the sound of three shots. This was soon followed by a loud howl which told him what had happened to his partner. The wolves had gotten him, and Henry was now on his own. With the two remaining dogs, he had to try to survive. Henry built a man harness and began to pull the sled himself. For days he would travel short distances, then stop well before nightfall. The first thing he did was to cut a large supply of lumber for the night's fire. This was always much greater than he would ordinarily need. With it he would build a huge fire and sit there trying to stay awake. After a time, it became increasingly difficult for him to do so. He would doze off, only to awake staring into the eyes of the wolf. Then he would take brands from the fire and fight off his enemy.

Finally one morning, Henry awoke to find himself surrounded by the wolf pack. Every time he made an attempt to move off, they would begin to close in on him. He needed the fire for protection, but he knew that he could not stay there forever. He did not like the thought of being breakfast for the hungry pack, but he was trapped. When one of the wolves made a rush for him, he threw a fire brand at it to drive it away.

He had to stay where he was and keep the fire going. However, that night he fell asleep in spite of himself. He had a dream that he was at Fort McGurry and that the fort was being attacked by wolves. The howling woke him, and he found himself actually being rushed by the pack. Jumping into the fire, he began to throw live coals at his attackers. This drove them back. Then he quickly built his fire in a circle and sat down in the middle of it. The wolves came to the outside edge, but they would not cross.

At daybreak, his fire was dwindling, but there was nothing he could do about it. Ready to give up, he sat down to sleep. However, when he awoke, the whole scene had changed. The wolves had disappeared. In their stead, there were four sleds and half a dozen men. Henry was saved.

Comment

In these three chapters, Jack London brings out the cunning of the savage animal. Notice how the she-wolf is the one who approaches the camp to lure the dogs away. Also in these chapter, the desolateness and the savagery of the wilderness are brought out. However, opposed to this is the intelligence of man. Henry, though desperate, saves himself by using his brain to outwit the animal. Thus the **theme** of this book is introduced to the reader.

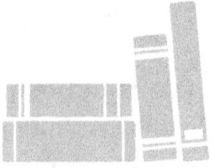

WHITE FANG

TEXTUAL ANALYSIS

CHAPTERS IV–VIII

In these chapters the author shows us the she-wolf in her own environment, the wild. After the pack was driven off by the newly-arrived men, the wolves ran off in search of other food. After a while they divided up into groups with each going its own way. The she-wolf was the object of the admiration of three males, but she would allow none of them to come near her. Finally, one of them, an old one-eyed wolf, using trickery, conquered and killed the other two. Thus he became the she-wolf's sole suitor. Together they ran off into the wilderness. These two became mates and hunted for food together.

During their travels they caught other animals for food. When they came upon the Indian lairs or traps, it was she who taught him how to raid them. After some time together, the she-wolf began to grow heavy. She became irritable, for it was almost time for her to have her litter. The two mates found a nest where the mother could deliver her young. When One-eye came back from hunting one day, he found five young cubs in the nest. However, the mother would not allow him to come near them. She knew by instinct that male wolves had been known to eat their own young. His only job, as far as she was concerned, was to get food for his family. She would reward him for this by a show of affection, but he could not come near the cubs.

During the time that followed, the cubs were fed with food brought by their father. Food became scarce and all but one gray cub died from hunger. In those hard times, even the mother wolf would go out in search of food. One time when the she-wolf was out, the young cub wandered away from the nest. The world of light was new to him as he stumbled along in these strange surroundings. Quite by accident the young cub fell upon a nest of ptarmigan chicks. After a few minutes, during which he satisfied his curiosity about his finding, he began to eat the chicks. However, coming away from the nest, he was attacked by the mother ptarmigan. Fiercely she fought him, and almost had him conquered when a hawk swooped down upon her and, luckily for the cub, carried his enemy away. The cub did not know what to make of it, but once delivered, he wandered on his way again.

A little later he came upon a baby weasel. As he was playing with it, the mother weasel appeared. Carrying the baby to safety, she quickly returned to attack the cub. Had it not been for the she-wolf's appearance on the scene, the mother weasel would have killed the cub. However, the she-wolf managed to save her cub by destroying the enemy.

During another time of famine, the she-wolf was again desperate for food. There was a lynx nest nearby, but she had carefully avoided it. The lynx is a vicious animal when attacked, and the wolf was no match for it. When One-eye had gone to this nest, he had been killed. The she-wolf knew this, but so great was her need that she was driven to raid it. That night, after she had eaten four of the kittens herself and had brought one back for her cub, the lynx came to the wolf nest for revenge. A fierce battle followed in which the cub helped his mother. Together they killed the fierce enemy. However, for days after, the she-wolf lay wounded and exhausted from the fight.

Comment

In these chapters, the author brings out the savagery of the wild. Animals kill other animals for food. However, although London spares no words in showing the viciousness of the animals, he also illustrates their virtue of mother-love. Notice how the mother wolf shields her young and endangers herself to save them, how the ptarmigan attacks the cub which had raided its nest and lastly, the revenge that the mother lynx seeks for the death of her litter. There is a law of the wilderness that says "eat or be eaten." But there are also instincts like that of the mother who risks her own life to protect her young.

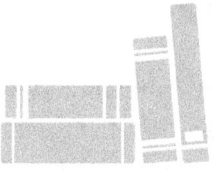

WHITE FANG

TEXTUAL ANALYSIS

CHAPTER IX

In this chapter the cub meets man for the first time. With the curiosity of the young which he first showed in the earlier chapters, the cub was again out roaming about. Without realizing it, he stumbled into the camp of some Indians. Half frightened, he did not know what to do when the Indian, Gray Beaver, came near him. However, when his mother came running into the camp after him, he felt reassured. But suddenly a voice yelled out "Kiche," and his mother obediently lay down. It develops that the she-wolf was really half dog and had run away from Gray Beaver's brother. Both mother and cub were claimed by him.

The cub was now given the name of White Fang and was kept in the camp with the men. He was soon to learn the ways of man and of his tame dogs. He got his first lesson in this when the dogs came back to camp and immediately attacked him. He was saved, however, by the men who beat their dogs off.

During the time that followed, White Fang began to learn some of the ways of man. His first experience was with fire, a thing which he had never seen before. After Gray Beaver made one, the cub walked over to do some examining. Thinking it was something harmless, he tested it in the same way he tested everything else. He tried to smell and to taste it. Of course, he was burned. This did not hurt him as much as the embarrassment, for he became a laughing stock to the men in the camp. White Fang also made an enemy in the camp. The pup Lip-lip had seemed friendly enough to him. However, when he approached the dog in this manner, Lip-lip struck out at him. The wolf cub was no match for the bigger, stronger animal, and so he fled to Kiche's protection. A bitter feud began at this point in the story.

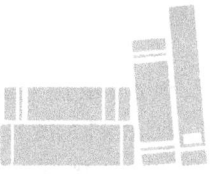

WHITE FANG

TEXTUAL ANALYSIS

CHAPTER X

White Fang began to learn a few of the more difficult things about living in civilization. For one thing, Kiche was tied lest she run away again. Thus White Fang could not depend upon her for protection unless he was by her side. However, he did pull one shrewd stunt on Lip-lip. He got the other dog to chase him. Then he ran around the camp for a while. Suddenly, he darted and ran past the place where his mother was tied. As Lip-lip passed in pursuit, Kiche grabbed him and avenged her cub. After that event, Lip-lip was very careful about attacking White Fang.

When the fear that she would run away was gone, Kiche was allowed to roam untied. Seeing that his mother was free, White Fang tried to persuade her to run away with him. However she would not go. Kiche had a new-found sense of satisfaction among men, and she did not want to leave them.

White Fang learned another difficult lesson, and it was that he could not stay with his mother. Gray Beaver owed a debt to

Three Eagles, and Kiche was given in payment. When the Indian started to take her away, White Fang insisted on following. He even swam out after the canoe, and Gray Beaver had to go out to get him back. White Fang had to be beaten in order to get him to return. But the laws of men were gradually being impressed on the wild dog. He was learning obedience to his master. He was becoming part of the tame world.

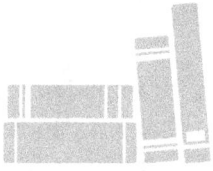

WHITE FANG

TEXTUAL ANALYSIS

CHAPTERS XI-XII

....

With his mother gone, White Fang now had no one to turn to for help. Lip-lip was his enemy; and the other dogs, who were the friends of Lip-lip, also became his enemies. White Fang became an outcast. He was not an accepted part of the camp, and yet he was forced to stay there. He was constantly in fights, often against great odds. No dog save Lip-lip dared attack him single-handedly. White Fang also got a bad reputation among the men. He stole food where and when he could. However, he was also blamed for everything that went wrong, even when he was not at fault. He was learning that in order to survive in the camp he had to be crafty both in the ways of the men and in those of the dogs. Man was his master. The dogs his size or bigger were his enemies. Those smaller were to be destroyed whenever he could get the chance to do so.

When the fall came, the Indians began to break up their summer camp in order to go off for their hunting. White Fang deliberately planned to stay behind. He watched for his opportunity to slip out of camp. Then he hid himself and did not answer Gray Beaver's calls for him. After a while he found himself alone in the forest. For a time this was good for him; but as the day began to fade, he realized that he was hungry. Camp life had softened him. Here there was no one to give him food nor any place to steal it. He realized his mistake and began to seek the new camp. This was difficult because he did not know the country. However, he did eventually find it. When he entered the camp, White Fang crawled on his belly to the feet of Gray Beaver. He expected a beating. Instead, the Indian gave him a piece of his own tallow to eat. Then he gave him some meat. White Fang had made his act of acceptance. Man was his acknowledged master.

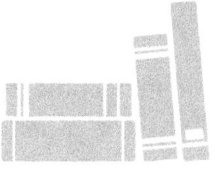

WHITE FANG

TEXTUAL ANALYSIS

CHAPTER XIII

....

When December came, Gray Beaver took a journey up the Mackenzie. With him went Mit-sah and Kloo-kooch. In order to help carry the load, Mit-sah was given a small sled and the puppies to pull it. White Fang was put into the harness for the first time, but he did not resent it. He had seen the other dogs work for their masters, and thus he was willing.

A fan-shaped harness was arranged so that the inexperienced dogs would not have to run directly behind each other. Mit-sah had much of the wisdom of his father. He had seen the mistreatment that White Fang had received from Lip-lip and now Mit-sah was in a position to avenge it. First, he put Lip-lip in the lead position. In this way, the other dogs would get the impression that they were chasing him, and he would become their enemy. Then he pretended to be rewarding Lip-lip for his good work. He would give him meat, but would not give any to the other dogs. This made them jealous of him. Gradually Lip-lip lost the position of leader which he had held among the younger dogs. In his place White Fang became a terrible task master. He had never been friendly with the other dogs, and now began to bully them into obedience.

On this trip White Fang performed a deed which endeared him to Gray Beaver. In the village of Great Slave Lake, he went out looking for scraps of food. When he saw a boy chopping some frozen moose meat, he began to lick up the splinters that had fallen to the ground. Then, for no apparent reason, the boy began to chase him. Finding himself cornered, White Fang had no choice but to attack the youth. This he did, biting him in his bid for freedom. When the boy's family demanded satisfaction, Gray Beaver would not give it to them. The Indian claimed that the boy attacked the dog unjustly. Later that day, Mit-sah was alone while gathering wood. The injured boy and some of his friends came and attacked him. At first, White Fang watched this, unconcerned. Then he realized that this was Mit-sah, his god, and rushed to the rescue. The attackers were scattered and Mit-sah saved.

White Fang was now established as the personal dog of Gray Beaver. He was given the important tasks to do. He had previously made his act of submission to the man. Now in exchange for the food, protection and companionship that Gray Beaver gave him, White Fang gave his liberty. He would do all that was required of him.

Comment

In these chapters note the use of the term god. Man is the god of the dog. In other words, he is the intelligent creature that guides his destiny. What London is trying to show is that the wild dog or wolf, if handled properly and taught to obey, will become the slave and helper of man.

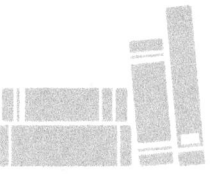

WHITE FANG

TEXTUAL ANALYSIS

CHAPTER XIV

....

When the group returned to the Indian camp to spend the summer, White Fang was one year old. Although he had not yet attained full growth, he was fully large enough to take care of himself. Baseek, an old dog, remembered White Fang for what he had been-the outcast of the camp. Thus at supper that first night, he tried to steal White Fang's food. At first, White Fang was frightened because he remembered how things were when he had been in camp before. But when he saw Baseek take a bite of his food, it was too much for him. White Fang attacked the old dog and drove him away. This was the last time that any of the other dogs tried to steal White Fang's food.

White Fang's second experience in camp was when he came upon Kiche. Suddenly he was face to face with her. He vaguely remembered his mother, but she did not know him at all. The female wolf soon forgets her young. Thus she drove him off. White Fang did not understand why she did this, but his wolf instinct told him that he should never fight the female of his breed. Thus he left her alone.

In the third year of White Fang's life, there came a great famine in the land. So great was it that the men ate the soft-tanned leather of their mittens and moccasins. The old and the weak died. Dogs ate other dogs, and even the men ate their dogs. White Fang retreated to the forest where he had had some experience. Here he was able to find enough food by hunting and by raiding the snares of the Indians. Once, finding a rabbit in Gray Beaver's snare, he even raided that. It did not matter to White Fang that his master was weak from hunger. During this stay in the forest, White Fang met Lip-lip who had also taken to the woods in search of food. However, he had not been as successful and was in poor condition. Thus White Fang attacked and very easily killed the dog who had persecuted him in the past. When White Fang returned to the camp some time later, he found that the famine was over.

Comment

The reader gets a further look at the savagery of the wilderness. Note, for example, the short way in which London disposes of Lip-lip. Suddenly the dog appears on the scene, and just as suddenly he is killed by White Fang.

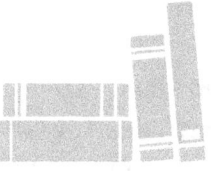

WHITE FANG

TEXTUAL ANALYSIS

CHAPTER XV

White Fang had never been liked by the dogs in the camp. However, when he was made leader of the dog team, they grew to hate him more intensely. They were jealous of the little extras that he received from Mit-sah. Such was their hatred that they would kill him if they could. However, the wolf in him made White Fang too wise for them and too quick. He would be upon them and then away before they could do anything to him. The effect on White Fang, though, was not good. He had the pride of leadership and conquest, but he was a sad and solitary dog. He was what is termed as a "loner," having no friends and desiring none.

In the summer, White Fang accompanied Gray Beaver to Fort Yukon. There had been rumors of the gold rush, and so the Indian came with bales of furs and gut-sewn mittens and moccasins. He had expected to make a large profit on them, but he had not expected the one thousand per cent that he was getting. While Gray Beaver was busy about his trading, White Fang had nothing to do. However, he found some entertainment for himself. This consisted of fighting the strange dogs that came off the steamers with the white men. White Fang had developed a vicious streak that he now gave free play. These new dogs from the South were afraid of the Wild to begin with, and were easy game for someone like White Fang. He could not, however, afford the risk of being blamed for killing them. To avoid this, he developed a trick of just wounding the dog and then leaving it. Thus, when other Indian dogs rushed in for the kill, it was they who got the blame for White Fang's misdeeds.

Comment

Again in this chapter Jack London paints a picture of wild savagery. However, in a sense, he tries to justify the actions of White Fang. After all, when White Fang first approached Lip-lip, he had done it in a friendly manner. Lip-lip was the one who had been unfriendly and who had turned the other dogs against the wolf cub. Also Gray Beaver had never shown any real affection for White Fang. True, he had made him the leader of the team and had given him a place of prominence in the camp, but the Indian had never shown any personal love for the wolf dog. Perhaps if he had, White Fang would have developed into a more kindly animal.

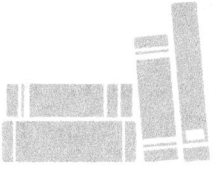

WHITE FANG

TEXTUAL ANALYSIS

CHAPTER XVI

....

There were only a few men who lived permanently in Fort Yukon. They called themselves Sour-dough's (referring to their bread which was made with sour-dough because they had no baking powder). The newcomers were called chechaquos. The men in the fort did not have much love for them and especially enjoyed the way White Fang and the gang of Indian dogs would attack the new dogs. They looked forward to the time when a steamer would come so that they could enjoy the fighting.

There was, however, one man who particularly enjoyed the sport. His name was Beauty Smith, but he was not called this for any good reason. Actually it was a joke name, for Beauty Smith was anything but beautiful. He was just the opposite, a monstrosity. His head was too big and his eyes protruded. But worse than his ugliness was the fact that he was a coward. The other men let him cook for them because someone had to do the job. They tolerated his presence, but they also feared him. Face to face he was not to be feared, but they never knew when he might shoot them in the back or poison their coffee.

Beauty Smith took a liking to White Fang. He admired the dog's strength and loved to see White Fang fight. Thus he determined to get him for himself. On the other hand, the wolf dog had nothing but hate for the man. When Beauty Smith came into Gray Beaver's camp, White Fang began to bristle. The white man offered the Indian money for the dog, but Gray Beaver had enough gold of his own. That is where the real treachery of Beauty Smith began to show itself. He started to bring whiskey to Gray Beaver. First he gave it to him, and then he began to sell it to him. Gradually he built up in the Indian a thirst for the whiskey. Soon Gray Beaver had spent all his money on it and the desire to drink was still there. Thus Beauty Smith got White Fang. He traded whiskey for the wolf dog.

However, White Fang went with the white man unwillingly. When he got his chance, he chewed the traces that held him and ran back to the camp of Gray Beaver. Again Beauty Smith took him and then beat him for running away. However, White Fang ran away a second time, and a second time Beauty Smith beat him. This time the whipping was so bad that the dog could hardly walk back to the fort. But White Fang now belonged to the white man. In order to make sure that he did not run away again, Beauty Smith chained him. Then Gray Beaver returned to the Indian camp without money and also without his dog.

Comment

The author paints a picture of human ugliness in this chapter. Gray Beaver had never shown White Fang any love, but he had always been fair with him. Thus the wolf dog, in its instinctive sense of loyalty, wanted to stay with its Indian master. But Beauty Smith has seen something he wants, and he uses a cowardly trick to get it. He makes a drunkard out of the Indian. A contrast is pictured here in this chapter. The reader cannot help but compare the loyalty of the wolf dog with the treachery of the man. The animal was instinctively loyal; whereas the man, who should know better, was evil.

WHITE FANG

TEXTUAL ANALYSIS

CHAPTERS XVII-XVIII

Once Beauty Smith got possession of White Fang, the true vicious nature of his character was revealed. The wolf dog was put into a pen and tormented. Beauty soon learned that the one thing White Fang hated most was to be laughed at. Thus he took every opportunity to embarrass the dog and then to laugh at it.

Up to the time that Beauty Smith entered his life, White Fang had been the enemy only of his own kind. Man was his god and his master. Now, however, all living creatures became his enemies. Worst of these was Beauty Smith. The abuse which the man heaped upon him did not make White Fang fear him. Actually the opposite was true. White Fang hated Beauty Smith, and it was only the club that the man carried that kept the wolf dog from killing him. Even when defeated by Beauty's club, White Fang would not cease growling at him.

White Fang was part dog and part wolf. On the one hand, he had the size of the big dog, and on the other, the cunning and the quickness of the wolf. He weighed a full ninety pounds, and all of it was muscle, bone, and sinew. Also he had a reputation as a fighter, and this was what Beauty Smith took advantage of. Dogs were brought to the pen and released in it. While men stood around cheering and betting, White Fang would tear his enemies apart. All sizes and types of dogs would be brought, but none could compare with the wolf dog. He was unconquerable. On one occasion, even a female lynx was put into the pen with White Fang. This was his greatest struggle, for her quickness and ferocity matched his. However, even in this fight he was successful. Soon all the fighting ceased because no match could be found for the great wolf dog, White Fang.

The inevitable happened, however. One day a faro dealer named Tim Keenan came into town with a bull dog. The squat fifty-pound dog was the ideal foe for White Fang. It was a type of dog not known in the Northland, and consequently, it would provide an interesting fight. When the dog was put into the pen with White Fang, it did not at first want to fight. Both animals were really confused, for neither knew what to make of the other. Finally, though, the fight did begin. But White Fang was in trouble because he did not know how to get at the bull dog with its short neck. All he could do was slash away. Meanwhile the bull dog kept stalking him. Finally, he grabbed White Fang's throat and just hung on. Nothing the wolf dog did could shake off the smaller animal. It looked as though the bull dog would choke the life right out of him. Beauty Smith even tried laughing at White Fang to make him more vicious, but this did not work. White Fang was too weak. The persistent bull dog would not let up.

Suddenly two men came on the scene. They had come up the trail. One rushed into the circle and tried to separate the two dogs. First, however, he had to knock Beauty Smith down in order to get him out of the way. Then his companion, a man named Matt, came in to help him, but the two still were unable to break the grip of the bull dog. Finally, the first man took his gun and used it on the bull dog's teeth as a pry. With this he was finally able to break the two dogs apart.

White Fang was nearly dead, but Beauty Smith was not angry at that. Instead he was angry because the fight had been stopped. The stranger, however, would take no nonsense from him. He forced Beauty to take one hundred and fifty dollars for White Fang. No one in the crowd dared interfere, for they knew that this was Weedon Scott, a special friend of the Gold Commissioner's.

Comment

In these chapters White Fang is driven almost insane by the insane Beauty Smith. There is savagery, but it is primarily on the part of the man. The dog is forced into it by being tormented. With Weedon Scott, however, a character who is truly civilized enters the story.

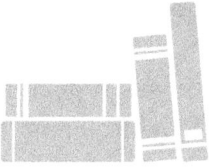

WHITE FANG

TEXTUAL ANALYSIS

CHAPTER XIX

When Weedon Scott and Matt got White Fang back to their cabin, they tried to calm him down. At first they were unsuccessful and White Fang had to be chained. For two weeks the men would argue. First one wanted to get rid of the wolf dog and the other didn't. Then the situation would reverse. Both really knew that White Fang was a good dog if they could only tame him. Finally Matt saw some marks on White Fang and realized that he had been tame before and that he had been in the harness. Then he convinced Scott that they should unchain the dog. Taking a club, Matt walked over and freed White Fang who remained where he was. But when the man threw him a piece of meat, another dog, Major, went after it. In a moment White Fang was upon him and the dog was dead. At this, Matt went to kick the wolf dog, but it was too fast for him. White Fang bit his leg. After this, Weedon Scott approached, trying to talk to him in a soothing voice. He got bitten on the hand for his trouble. Matt then went into the cabin and came out with the rifle. Seeing the gun, White Fang began to growl. As soon as Matt would set it down, the dog would stop growling. This was repeated a few times. Both men were convinced then that White Fang was too intelligent to be killed.

Comment

Matt and Weedon Scott are both truly civilized men. Yet, even with them there is a certain disregard for life. When White Fang kills Major, all the two men can say is that he deserved it. There is no sympathy for death.

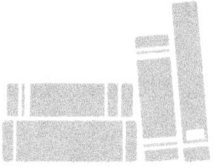

WHITE FANG

TEXTUAL ANALYSIS

CHAPTER XX

In this chapter the actual taming of White Fang takes place. Weedon Scott is determined that he will succeed in this. The day after the dog had bitten Scott's hand, the man went out with some chunks of meat. He went near White Fang and offered him some of the meat. However, the dog did not trust him enough to come to him, so Scott threw the meat to it. The man repeated this action several times until finally White Fang realized that this person was his friend. Then he actually ate the meat from Scott's hand. From this time the dog grew to like and then to love this man. With Gray Beaver it had been respect and loyalty that held White Fang. Here it was true affection on both sides.

Gradually the dog began to feel a change come over him. He became more and more like the other dogs around him, and less attracted to the wild. After a time Matt tried to harness him to the sled. At first White Fang refused; then Weedon Scott succeeded and everything was all right. After this, the wolf dog showed his power and soon became the leader of the team which feared and respected him.

When Weedon Scott left in the morning, White Fang would await his return all day. One time, however, Scott went out in the morning and did not return in the evening. He had had to go away. A surprising change took place in the attitude of White Fang. He brooded, ate little, would do no work and soon got sick for the first time in his life. Matt had to write to Scott and tell him what was happening. The other man returned as quickly as possible and once more White Fang was himself.

One night the two men heard a howl outside the cabin. When they went out, they found White Fang on top of a man, trying to gash his throat. After Scott and Matt got the dog away, they found that the man was Beauty Smith. He had come to try to kidnap White Fang. However, in return, he had almost gotten himself killed.

Comment

In this chapter Jack London demonstrates his **theme**. A wild wolf, if treated properly and shown love, will return the affection. There is no reason why the animal cannot be tamed. Everything depends upon the way in which the man handles the situation. The contrast in this chapter is brought out when Beauty Smith returns. White Fang almost kills him because he hates the treatment that the man had given him. On the other hand, White Fang himself almost dies of loneliness when Weedon Scott goes away.

WHITE FANG

TEXTUAL ANALYSIS

CHAPTERS XXI-XXIII

When it was time for Weedon Scott to return home, he planned to leave White Fang behind. The dog sensed what was going on.

However, Scott could not take a wolf into the Southland. Leaving for the steamer, the man locked the dog in the cabin. But, when he got to the dock, there was White Fang waiting for him. The animal had jumped through the window of the cabin in order to follow his master. With this display of love, Scott decided that he must take White Fang with him no matter what.

When the steamer landed in San Francisco, White Fang was frightened by what he saw. Never before in his life had there been anything like this. But it did not last long except in his memory. Soon he was on a train that was heading for Sierra Vista, the home of Judge Scott, Weedon's father. At the estate, a woman embraced Weedon and White Fang raised a howl. When he learned that this was Scott's mother and that she was not trying to hurt his master, the dog was satisfied. However, when he came upon a sheep dog, he began an attack. He stopped short in this, though, when he realized that the sheep dog was a female. But the sheep dog was not bound by the same law, and she made her attack. This was the first of a series of incidents with the sheep dog. She would attack him, but he would not fight back. His instincts told him not to fight a female, but hers told her to drive off the wolf. Later, at the house, he met another dog called Dick. Weedon stopped White Fang from fighting this one. He knew that the wolf dog would kill it.

At Sierra Vista, White Fang had much to learn. First he had to learn to respect all the members of his master's family. Then there were the servants who had to be obeyed. Next, White Fang had to learn a new way of life. He could not fight the dogs as he had done in the Northland. Also he must not kill the chickens or other animals that were kept by his master. When children in town laughed at him or threw stones, he had to ignore them. Lastly, when strange dogs chased him, he was not to fight them. All of this was difficult, but White Fang learned it gradually. There was one consolation he discovered. It was all right to chase jackrabbits, squirrels, and other animals such as these.

WHITE FANG

TEXTUAL ANALYSIS

CHAPTER XXIV

....

As time passed, White Fang became more and more civilized. However, only Weedon and his sister Beth had any faith in the wolf dog. The others in the family merely tolerated him and remained doubtful about his being tame. As far as the animals were concerned, he was never bothered by any of them except Collie. She was nagging at him all the time.

One of White Fang's great delights was to accompany Weedon Scott on his horseback rides. Being a wolf, he never tired of running beside the larger animal, and even fifty miles across the countryside was not too much for him. One day the horse tripped, spilling Weedon and causing him to break his leg. The man told White Fang to go home, but the dog was so devoted to him that he did not want to leave. Finally, Scott convinced him to go. The problem, however, was that once White Fang got home, he could not tell anyone what had happened. The only sounds he could make were a howl and a growl. Therefore, he tried everything he could think of to get some member of the family to come back with him. So violent did he become in his effort that he frightened them. Then, with one great effort, he rushed out a great burst of barking. With this, Weedon's wife Alice realized that something was wrong, and they all rushed out after the wolf dog.

One day during the next winter, White Fang realized that Collie's teeth were not so sharp as they had been in the past. When she nipped his ear and invited him to follow her, he ran off into the woods after her as One-eye had chased Kiche one day years before.

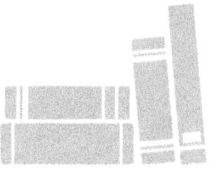

WHITE FANG

TEXTUAL ANALYSIS

CHAPTER XXV

The only one in the family who still remained a disbeliever about White Fang was old Judge Scott. This chapter is important to the novel only insofar as it relates how White Fang saved the Judge's life. A criminal named Jim Hall escaped prison one night. When Judge Scott had sentenced him, he swore that he would get revenge. However, no one at Sierra Vista was frightened except Alice. For this reason, she would bring White Fang into the house at night. Thus on the night that Jim Hall came to get the Judge, White Fang was there. In a vicious fight the wolf dog killed the invader but was himself seriously wounded. So happy was the Judge that his life had been saved that he gave White Fang the best care money could buy. This care plus the wolf dog's strong constitution served to restore him to health. After this incident, Alice called him the Blessed Wolf, and by this name was he known from then on. The novel concludes on a happy note. After White Fang recovered, he was brought outside to see the puppies he had fathered. In these puppies the Wild-White Fang-was united with the Tame-Collie. The story was complete. A wolf had been changed into a civilized dog.

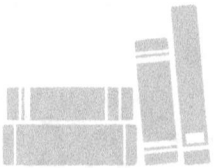

WHITE FANG

CHARACTER ANALYSIS AND THEME

There are many characters in the novel *White Fang*, but the only important ones are those which had a definite influence upon bringing out the **theme** of the story. Jack London was trying to show that an animal is influenced by its environment. This means that if he is in the Wild, he lives according to its rule of "eat or be eaten." If others are mean to it, the animal will be mean in return. However, when it receives love and kindly treatment, it will return love and loyalty.

KICHE AND LIP-LIP

They are important because the one teaches White Fang how to survive in the Wild, and the other provides him with a natural enemy. Kiche, the mother, has no characteristic other than that she is an animal who knows how to survive in spite of hardship. Lip-lip's only trait is meanness. He hates White Fang for no good reason. The two are natural enemies, and that is all the explanation the author gives.

GRAY BEAVER

This Indian represents the impersonal being. The dog is to him merely something which he uses. He neither loves it nor hates it. He will feed it and give it shelter, but he will not give it any personal love. In return he gets an impersonal loyalty. The dog White Fang is loyal to him and will work for him, but that is all.

BEAUTY SMITH

He represents the evil man. The animal exists only for his personal pleasure. He does not use it for work. He takes out his hatred for the world on the dog. All he wants to do is torment White Fang. He does not care if the dog lives or dies. He does not even care if the dog hates him. The only thing he wants in return for feeding the dog is the money he can get by having White Fang fight. Consequently, he receives the dog's hatred in return for this.

WEEDON SCOTT

He is important because he represents the kind of man who loves animals. White Fang is to him another creature. This animal must be shown affection and shown that he is needed. He is not just something to be worked. The animal is for companionship and love. In return for this attitude, White Fang gives Weedon Scott his love and undying loyalty. The wolf changes his whole outlook on life because of this man. From a wild, fighting beast, he becomes a tame, civilized dog.

WHITE FANG

He, of course, is the most important character of all. It is through him that the author develops his **theme**. We see him change from the wild wolf to the tame wolf dog; then into a vicious beast; and lastly into a tame dog of the Southland.

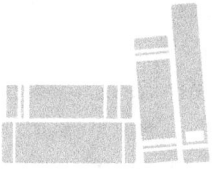

WHITE FANG

ESSAY QUESTIONS AND ANSWERS

Question: What are some of the qualities, good or bad, of the novel *White Fang*?

Answer: The novel *White Fang* is an interesting dog story. It is clearly and simply written so that a person can easily read it. There are no obscure passages and no difficult passages in it. Like *The Call of the Wild* it is a naturalistic novel, but the message is too obvious and the author keeps pointing it out to the reader. Also like *The Call of the Wild* it is a romantic tale of the Northland. However, the magic that the other novel contains is not found in *White Fang*. Unfortunately, the adventure and romance is too often dulled by the constant, seemingly unnecessary, acts of savagery. Also, although the characterization is well done for the purpose of the author's theme, the characters themselves are too typical. They do not stand out as individuals.

Question: The first three chapters seem to have little connection with the novel. What is their significance?

Answer: The first three chapters of this book set the mood of the novel. The story of the two men out in the frozen wilderness and surrounded by the wolves creates the impression of desolation so important to the novel. However, this story also creates a picture of London's own little world. To the author, Bill and Henry are the human race. The wilderness is the world and the wolves are the forces of nature. The fact that the wolves are using every trick to get the men means that the forces of nature are trying to destroy mankind. Furthermore, Bill is the impatient man who can't wait. He rushes out to meet nature on her own ground. Consequently, he is destroyed as the wolves eat him. On the other hand, Henry is the patient man. He waits for nature to attack him. When she does, he uses fire-one of nature's own forces-to defeat her. As a result, he survives. Throughout the novel, savagery is fought with savagery in the wilderness.

Question: Contrast the character of Beauty Smith with that of Weedon Scott.

Answer: Beauty Smith is hardly a beautiful man. In fact, Jack London goes into great detail to describe the ugliness of this man. Beauty is really no more than a beast. He is mean and vicious. Whatever pain he can inflict on White Fang, or on any one else for that matter, he enjoys. If *White Fang* were a story of good and evil, we would say that Beauty Smith was the symbol of evil. However, since it is not a story of good and evil, we might perhaps say that Beauty Smith represents the animal in man.

On the other hand, the author spends very little time in describing the physical appearance of Weedon Scott. This character is somewhat handsome. He is also patient and kind. But these facts we learn more by their being implied than by London actually telling them to us. Weedon Scott then represents the civilized in man: he is man's better self.

CRITICAL COMMENTARY

EARLY CRITICISM

Ninetta Eames Payne, the first person ever to write about Jack London, said of him: "If this youthful California writer makes a study of literary style, it is not apparent, so simply and unaffectedly does he relate a story. This young man of twenty-four has something more vital to offer than finish . . . he reaches the humanity of his readers by direct course." These words, printed in the *Overland Monthly* for May, 1900, probably sum up the style of Jack London as well as any others which have ever been written about him. Always is he simple, direct and to the point. There is no straining after good sentence structure or beautiful, poetic language. London had a message to deliver, and he spoke it clearly. So successful was he that in the years between 1900 and 1916 he was the best paid and wealthiest writer in America.

LONDON AS "HACK"

However, in spite of the glowing praise of Ninetta Eames Payne, and in spite of the warm reception that he received from the reading public, he was not generally considered by the critics of his times to be a good writer. The term "hack" was often applied to him because of the number of stories he was able to turn out for the magazines. Also many critics called him a writer of the sensational because he identified himself with the problems of the muck-rakers of his time, as did writers like Upton Sinclair, and with the socialist movement that was going on in America at the turn of the century.

CONTEMPORARY CRITICISM

Edward Wagenknecht in Cavalcade of the American Novel tells us that for Jack London writing was never more than a means to an end and that end was material advancement. In other words, he wrote because it was the best way he knew to make money. He liked strong words rather than precise language. He tried to keep himself out of his writing, tried to let the characters tell the story by their deeds and actions. Although the characteristics of his style are simplicity and fluency, he is sometimes clumsy and very often repetitious. He very seldom was careful with his work. The stories never give the impression of his having spent much, if any, time trying to revise them. However, he had a message to deliver-that of atavism-and he did it with fair success in *White Fang* and *The Call of the Wild*. To quote Wagenknecht, "He was a hack writer of some genius, and, as has been said of Byron, the faults of his works were the faults of his life."

LONDON AND VIOLENCE

Alfred Kazin points out that violence is the keynote of London's works. He was not always writing as a deliberate hack. He did not believe that any strength was equal to his own, and he tries to show this in many of his works. The characters live by violence, for the world is the testing ground of the strong. But, through all of his plots, London, the seaman and adventurer, comes out.

Even in Buck's return to the wild, Kazin reminds us, there is Jack London's yearning for a return to the time when life was a wild man-to-man struggle.

NATURALISM AND STYLE

There is no doubt in the minds of most critics that Jack London is one of the good story tellers in American Literature. However, having been born in an age when our literature was still in its infancy, he had no great literary tradition upon which to fall back for help. Consequently, he turned elsewhere for guidance in his philosophy of writing. One of the European authors he selected was the Frenchman, Emile Zola. This author was a great advocate of naturalism. This is the theory that the novelist is like the scientist. The novel is a laboratory experiment. The author selects some social or philosophical theory and tries it out on his characters, while he himself remains impersonal. He does not enter into the story, but merely stands by and watches for the results. London tried to imitate this style, but he was not this type of person. He had lived much of what he wrote about; therefore, he found it difficult to be impersonal. Also he found it difficult not to preach. Many of his novels suffer because of these faults. His works become uninteresting because they are merely sermons in which the author gives his personal feelings about the subject. John Barleycorn, his novel about drunkenness, is a good example of this fault. In it are many of the author's own personal experiences with the alcohol problem. Then also, this book is a plea for Prohibition.

THE PROBLEM OF ACTION

Another difficulty that Jack London had in his writing was that he found it difficult to sustain the action of his stories. *The Call of the Wild*, probably his best novel, is good, but it is also short and episodic. *The Sea Wolf*, the novel in which he tried to develop the theory of atavism as it applied to a man, begins well. When the conflict concerns Wolf Larsen and Humphrey Van Weydan, the novel succeeds. However, when the character of Maud, the woman, enters, the plot begins to falter, and the story ends as a desert island romance. Thus it is generally agreed among the critics that it is among London's shorter works that we find his better ones. His short stories, like "To Build a Fire" and "All Gold Canyon," are gems of good storytelling.

As yet there has been no complete edition or edited works of Jack London published. Until such time as this might be done, it is difficult to assign Jack London his correct place in American literature. However, we do know that he does deserve a place. As Alfred Kazin says of him, "If he seems to be slipping away even as a boy's hero, he remains significant because his work is a feverish concentration of all the insurgence and obsession with power that came to the fore in the Progressive period."

BIBLIOGRAPHY

Biography

Charmian London, *The Book of Jack London*, New York: Century Press, 1921.

Richard O'Connor, *Jack London, A Biography*, Boston: Little, Brown & Co., 1964.

Irving Stone, *Sailor on Horseback*, Boston: Houghton-Mifflin Co., 1938.

Critical Study

Frederick Feied, *No Pie in the Sky: The Hobo as American Cultural Hero in the Works of Jack London*, John Dos Passos, and Jack Kerouac, New York: Citadel Press, 1964.

Alfred Kazin, *On Native Grounds*, New York: Doubleday & Co. Inc., 1956.

Spiller, Thorp, Johnson, & Canby, "Towards Naturalism in Fiction," in *Literary History of the United States*, New York: The Macmillan Co., 1958.

Edward Wagenknecht, *Cavalcade of the American Novel*, New York: Holt, Rinehart, & Winston, 1952.

Philosophy

Arthur Masiello, *Darwinism in the Works of Jack London*, a thesis on file in the library of Seton Hall University, South Orange, 1960.

Edward Biron Payne, *The Soul of Jack London*, Kingsport: Southern Publishers, Inc., 1933.

www.ingramcontent.com/pod-product-compliance
Lightning Source LLC
LaVergne TN
LVHW011729060526
838200LV00051B/3085